CHILDHOOD
IT SHOULD
NOT *HURT!*

A GUIDE FOR THOSE CONCERNED
WITH OUR CHILDREN'S HEALTH AND
WELFARE

Claire R. Reeves

LTI Publishing
Interactive And Innovative Publications
THE FUTURE IS INTERACTIVE™

Printed in the United States of America
Distributed by LTI Publishing

LTI Publishing, Inc.
P.O. Box 371
Huntersville, NC 28070
Email: Art@LTIPublishing.net

Editors:Claudia Suzanne, Dr. Michael Meyer
Cover/Book Designer: David A. Jones

Library of Congress Catalog Card Number: 2003109979

Publisher's Cataloging in Publication
(*Prepared by LTI Publishing, Inc.*)

ISBN 0-9743048-0-8

- To hold adults accountable for abusing them or allowing abuse to continue.

- To enjoy the same legal and constitutional rights adults enjoy.

- To have a guardian advocate oversee the work of the system exclusively for them.

- To have legal matters pertaining to their protection heard by a judge other than the one presiding over their parents' divorce.

- To have their case heard by a judge trained and experienced in the full effects of child sexual abuse and child development.

- To hold an accused parent responsible for proving visitation would be good for the child, rather than hold the protecting parent responsible for proving it might cause harm.

- To see their convicted abusers punished under the full extent of the law rather than have sentences mitigated because the victim was a child or family member.

- To be examined by doctors and experts who have extensive experience and training in child-sexual-abuse issues.

To my son, Arthur Francis Cooksey, III.

A dedication page is not enough to properly thank this young man for his years of dedication to MASA and his belief in the importance of this book. Art has been my greatest champion in helping child-sexual-abuse victims. Although never a victim himself, after meeting so many survivors of child sexual abuse through MASA, he became a crusader in the fight to stop this abuse. I am so proud to be his mom.

MOTHERS AGAINST SEXUAL ABUSE (MASA) is dedicated to educating society about this horrific abuse of our children, and to helping survivors reclaim their lives. Hopefully, *Childhood It Should Not Hurt* will help speed the healing process.

Our message to child victims and adult survivors: There is no "quick fix," but with encouragement and belief in your own wonderful human spirit, you can reclaim your life and move forward.

Our message to those caught in the quagmire of the court systems: Know that all is not lost. as our judges, social workers, law enforcement officials and others connected to the courts become more educated about the evils of child sexual abuse, the tide will turn in your favor. You must not give up. Everything depends on your courage and tenacity. You can and you will persevere.

Acknowledgements

I could easily fill a book with the names of the wonderful and dedicated people who have not only supported the publishing of this book, but also MOTHERS AGAINST SEXUAL ABUSE (MASA) for so many years.

First and foremost, I would like to thank Claudia Suzanne who believed in the book when it was only an idea. Claudia has been involved in every aspect of the production of the book and has guided me through the difficult material. When my words were too accusatory, Claudia reworked them to be palpable to judges and other professionals who need to be educated, not blamed. Every writer should be fortunate enough to have a Claudia Suzanne.

Dr. Michael Meyer dissected every line for clarity and readability as well as legal issues. Thank you Mike! You caused me to do many rewrites, but our mutual goal was to provide an understandable, easy-to-read book.

David Jones, a former animator for *The Simpsons* television show, designed the book's cover, offered emotional support and encouragement and strongly shares my dedication to protecting children. Thank you, David, for your constant enthusiasm on this important project.

Glenda Burns, dear friend and colleague, spent hours researching the bibliography and alphabetizing everything.

Donald D'Haene, friend, fellow Canadian and author of *Father's Touch*, provided support and Canadian marketing ideas that will enhance the book's visibility in my native country.

A special thank you to the angel investors who believed enough in this book to risk their hard-earned money. You are deeply appreciated. Many children will receive the help they need because of you. If the whole world got together and thanked you at once, that would not be enough.

I also want to express my deepest appreciation to the MASA supporters whose dedication has allowed our organization to continue. The following is not in alphabetical order, nor does it encompass all our dedicated supporters:

Al and Susan Jarreau. Ronnie Lippin, Lou and May Steinberg and Phil Sheldon, CEO, of Survivors and Victims Empowered. Jackie Lichtenstein, M.D., Douglas J. Wolf, Esq., Gloria Allred, Esq., former California Assemblywoman Paula Boland, Anna Miranda, Arlene Drake, Ph.D., Charlene and Duane Marks, Polly Sweenie, Dorothy Linnebur, Jack Linnebur, Jo Bates, Nina Salerno, Anna Miranda, Alex Lujan, Justin Rancor, Johnny Santos *(Lead Singer, SPINE-SHANK)*, Shari Karney, Esq., Jeffrey Bennett, Sue Griffith, Psy.D., John E. B. Myers, Esq., Bob Rinear, Lisa Bloom, Esq., Lisa Davimos, Deann Tilton Durfee, Donna Friess, Ph.D., Honorable Ken Friess, Mark E. Roseman, Esq., Seth Goldstein, Esq., Paul Griffith, Donna Huhem, Greg Willis, Candace Lightner, (Founder of MADD), Susan Carpenter McMillan, Amy Neustien, Ph.D., Detective Robert Navarro, retired LAPD., Roland Summit, M.D., Suzanne Thompson, Thomas E. Wall, esq., Nina Salerno, Laurie Johnson, Carol Webb, Pam Perskins, Randy Noblitt, Ph.D., Charlotte Blasier, Bill York, Liz Lincoln, Margaret Kennedy, Deanna Smith, Loretta Woodbury, Catherine Gould, Ph.D., Vicky Costain, Ph.D., Gwen and Gary Dean, Ph.D., Lynn Forrester, Ph.D., Bobbi Carlson, Ph.D., June Dunbar, Howard Temaner, Ph.D., Anette Powell, Patrycia Perez, Rachel Taylor, former governor Pete Wilson and former attorney general Dan Lungren.

The above is by no means a complete list. My most heartfelt thanks and appreciation goes out to every person who has joined in the crusade to stop the sexual abuse of children.

TOM ECONUMUS, THE LINKUP

(For those abused by priests)

LAUREN STRATFORD

(Author and advocate for survivors)

JUNE DUNBAR

(Advocate for the rights of women and children)

DAN SEXTON

(Advocate for survivors)

I truly know if there is a cause in heaven the four of you are fighting for it and shaking things up. We all miss you so much.

STILL REACHING

By Patrycia Perez

I see endless sky & ocean
as I sit upon the sand.

I know there is an ending
but I don't see from where I am.

The ocean can be deadly
but I'm safe upon the shore.

Yet I hear my name called faintly
amidst the ocean roar.

Pass the ocean waves,
quietly beyond,

There upon still waters
I hear amazing songs.

Slowly I make footprints
deep within the sand,

Gaining strength and wisdom;
learning how to stand.

And every step is progress,
not one stride alone.

As God's resounding whispers
become my stepping stone

Having spent a decade as a psychiatric nurse followed by twenty years as an FBI agent investigating violent crimes, I saw first-hand the devastating effects child sexual abuse has on our society. From the first moment of a child's violation, their innocence untimely and selfishly taken, we all suffer a loss. Oftentimes the victims of this shameful crime, as well as their family and their community suffer a second victimization at the hands of an inept and overburdened social-service agency and criminal-justice system— or should I say criminal injustice system? But does it have to be that way? Do we have to accept the status quo (reunification of abused child with parent) that allows, even encourages, helpless victims to be denied salvation?

Claire Reeves, president and founder of Mothers Against Sexual Abuse (MASA) says "NO! We do not!" In her new book *CHILDHOOD...It Should not Hurt*, Reeves takes a highly comprehensive look at all aspects of this issue, including how to tell if your child has been (or is being) violated, case studies of child victims and adult survivors of child sex abuse, the failings of child-protective agencies and the oftentimes outrageous decisions by the court system, why "Reunification" rarely works, and what we as private citizens can do about it. This book should serve as a "Bible" for anyone who works with or even cares about our children, our future.

Candice Rosing DeLong, Author

Special Agent: My Life on the Front Lines as a Woman in the FBI

It is late; the household is quietly sleeping. Footsteps pad down the hall and stop outside a closed door. The door slowly opens, and the big man moves silently across the room to the bed where a seven-year-old, tightly curled into the fetal position, lies crying. Making soft cooing noises, the man drops his robe and crawls into the bed with the child.

Are you horrified? Disgusted? Sickened at the very thought?

Just think what the seven-year-old is feeling.

Nothing would make me happier than to admit the above scenario is a product of my imagination—but it isn't. This horror is reenacted daily in households all over the country on an equal-opportunity basis; incest and child sexual abuse know no social, financial, political, racial or religious bounds. In fact, the latest statistics released from the Department of Justice tell us that one out of three girls and one out of four boys will be sexually violated one or more times before reaching age eighteen.

Is your child one of them?

Were you?

According to a 1993 Los Angeles Times survey, more than fifty-eight million American women are adult survivors of incest and child sexual abuse. The enormity of that number is staggering. It is especially staggering when you consider that the article only mentioned female victims of child sexual abuse. When you consider the statistics for male survivors, it is almost unbelievable.

A more recent four-part Times study found that 63-67% of unwed teenage mothers were incest victims. Over 80% of the mother's of today's incest victims were also victimized when they were children.

You must be wondering how these statistics can be true, but it is not that difficult to calculate the frightening numbers. Over 85% of all perpetrators are adults the child knows and trusts.

But here's the most frightening statistic of all: over 50% of the children whose parents are involved in Family and Dependency custody cases are returned to the sole custody of the parent accused of abuse.

The stories in this book are all true. The names have been changed to protect privacy.

CONTENTS

In our society, as in many cultures, "family" has always been considered sacrosanct—whatever happens in the family is private. However, when dysfunctional family members spill over into an innocent society and cause harm, it seems to me it is everyone's affair.

We live in a country where almost anyone can earn a living and lifestyles are the highest in the world, yet crime rates are soaring and our jails are full-to-overflowing. Where are all these criminals coming from?

We have all heard the "Abuse Excuse": he robbed the liquor store because his mother used to beat him; she murdered her kids because her father raped her when she was five. This defense is used so routinely that it has become standard fodder for media talking heads, who jeer and vilify it. Nevertheless, studies bear it out: over 90% of all inmates in this country were abused children. They are what I call "non-survivors." They never learned how to overcome the dysfunction of their childhood and reclaim their lives.

Many people over the years have asked me how I can work with such an issue as child sexual abuse—it is so depressing and upsetting. My answer has always been, "If it is depressing and upsetting for me as an adult, what must it be for the little child who is experiencing the abuse?" But the truth goes much deeper than that.

A PERSONAL ISSUE

Incest and child sexual abuse were not issues I knew anything about for most of my life. They simply did not exist in my world or the world of my acquaintances and friends. If I ever thought about incest—which was almost never—I thought about two first cousins getting married.

Then I found out it was happening in my own family.

My initial reaction was denial. I later found out that denial is most people's first reaction. In my case, I knew of no other family that had this kind of problem, and I had no idea how to handle it. There was little written matter on the subject, and most of that was couched in highly clinical terms. In fact, the consensus at the time was that only one out of a million families experienced the tragedy of incest. Based on those statistics, I deduced that I was crazy to think this could be happening in our upper-middle-class family.

It was happening.

Confronting the ugliness of the truth was excruciatingly painful, but I quickly realized that if it could happen in my family, it could happen in any family. That knowledge changed my destiny.

A former journalist, I researched every aspect of child sexual abuse. The minute information available gave little assistance to a family in crisis. I persevered.

I needed to speak with actual victims. I still thought—and hoped—I could be wrong, and that there really weren't many youngsters and families who even knew about this kind of abuse, let alone were affected by it. At the time, I was living in Toronto, a city I still consider my hometown. I placed an advertisement in a leading magazine asking for victims of child sexual abuse to contact me. I thought I might receive a few scattered calls.

The response was overwhelming. Survivors of sexual abuse from Newfoundland to Vancouver, British Columbia called to share their childhood tragedies. These brave individuals were my first inclination that I was delving into a rampant and very real problem.

I discovered that literally thousands of lives had been torn apart by this unspeakable crime as I unintentionally created a Canadian following. I was the lady who knew and believed and validated victims of incest.

Unfortunately, belief and validation was all I could give them; I had neither the education nor expertise to do any more at the time. I promised to write an expose on their behalf if the opportunity ever presented itself.

The survivors thanked me and encouraged me to seek the truth for them. They were the first cheerleaders in my quest to uncover this crippling devastation of the most innocent and helpless victims of evil self-indulgence.

I researched and wrote and researched some more. I moved to California to be closer to my son and to write a book. Another newspaper advertisement brought another overwhelming response. I spent most of 1991 conducting interviews, including over forty convicted child molesters. All the interviews were taped, and I began to think I would need a warehouse to store them. Something needed to be done to ease the pain and suffering of the innocent victims.

In March 1992, I awoke one morning with the name MASA on my lips and a great sense of urgency to do something to help. That was the moment I decided to found an organization to help victims of incest and child sexual abuse, and to tell the world about this terrible crime.

Mothers Against Sexual Abuse (MASA) was founded March 25, 1992. We did indeed become a voice for the victims. This book is also a voice for the victims, and fulfills the promise I made so many years ago: to expose this most secret and prolific crime against the most innocent, our children.

IRRETRIEVABLE LOSS

Did you know that the first high-profile child-abuse case in this country had to be investigated by the Society For the Prevention of Cruelty to Animals? That was over sixty years ago, and its handling became the template for today's social-service agencies that are supposed to protect children.

Something is terribly wrong, when some sixty years later the societies to protect animals are still greater and more influential than the societies to protect our children.

As a dedicated animal lover and owner, I am all for saving endangered species and stopping the abuse of little four-legged creatures. I would just like to see children get equal time and protection.

Our social service agencies are failing miserably in their efforts to protect children. They claim children who receive little protection and care "fall through the cracks." After the many years I have worked in this field, I think "falling into the abyss" is a more appropriate phrase. We are losing too many children, and too many are beyond help even if and when we discover the errors that were made in their cases.

Our current legal system places far too much emphasis on the rights of the parents and far too little on the rights of the children. When reunification became a Federal Mandate in 1985, the theory was that by assisting troubled families and teaching abusive parents to become loving protectors of their children, reunited families would live happily ever after.

Children were taken into protective custody and put into foster care. The abusive parents were court ordered to attend parenting classes, substance-abuse treatment, anger management classes and other therapeutic interventions with the aim of becoming good and loving parents. It sounded so good on paper.

Unfortunately, paper isn't reality. The parental requirements were minimal, and the established timeline for their rehabilitation was one year. Either the abusive parent shaped up in a year, or a Termination of Parental Rights case plan would be initiated.

The definition of "shaping up" turned out to be nothing more than attending the prescribed classes and treatments, not an actual change in behavior or attitude.

REUNIFICATION TRAGEDY

A mother perpetrated sexual abuse and gross neglect to two beautiful little girls. The oldest, aged six, had tuberculosis when she was taken into protective custody and the youngest had suffered a dog bite while visiting one of the mother's boyfriends. The mother had sought no medical care for the youngest child and refused to identify the boyfriend or provide information about the dog. Consequently, the child had to undergo a series of painful rabies shots.

The mother had a history of alcohol and drug abuse and was on probation for driving while under the influence. She also had a history of severe domestic violence and assault perpetrated against numerous boyfriends. In one instance, she had burned down the boyfriend's home and threatened his children. Her criminal record also included forgery and other felonies.

Despite this extensive criminal and abuse background, this mother was considered a candidate for reunification with her children. She ignored all of the court orders for the first sixty days after her children were taken into protective custody, and in one instance, appeared in court intoxicated.

In the third month, the mother began to comply with some of the court orders. She attended a parenting class and an outpatient treatment center for alcohol and drug abuse. She sporadically attended Alcoholics Anonymous. Serious recovery requires ninety meetings in ninety days; she didn't even come close. Nevertheless, she met the minimal requirements for the reunification process.

Most of the people involved in this case became ecstatic. Mom became a hero because she had cleaned up for a few months, and social services could point to another reunification success story.

IS SUCCESS PROBABLE?

This particular case is so convoluted there is no way to cover all the incidents. The oldest child's father had passed away, leaving a monthly income from Social Security for his daughter. The mother had already defrauded the Social Security Administration by falsely swearing that the deceased father of her oldest child was also her youngest child's father. That fraud was discovered when the mother sued another man for child support of the younger girl, and paternity tests were taken. The man sued for paternity was also not the father.

Is it possible the mother made an effort to meet the minimal reunification requirements so she could get her daughter's Social Security benefit?

Is it possible that social services could be so blind as to not notice that possibility?

Whatever the incentive, the court will be removing the two girls from the foster-care home in which they were thriving to once again live with a mother who has met the very minimal legal standards for parenting over the bare minimum period of one year.

When the mother once again proves that she did not have enough time in recovery or enough parenting education to provide safety and security for her children, they will likely be removed again and returned to the system. They had been in an adoptive foster-care home where they received love, safety and security for the first time in their lives. The next time, they may not be so fortunate. They could easily be shuttled from foster home to foster home, and even get separated from each other. It is my most earnest hope that the mother has indeed healed and can provide a safe and healthy home for her children. The saddest part of this case is that the children are the litmus to measure success or failure. My personal opinion is that the price for the children is too high.

THIS BOOK IS A CALL FOR CHANGE

When a parent is abusive and neglectful from the time of birth, any and all consideration should be given only to the best interests of the child. The parent should be held accountable and encouraged to make life changes; in all likelihood, he or she was also abused. Nevertheless, the child should be the first consideration.

If a child is placed into a good and loving family, the parent's rights should be the very last consideration. Parental Rights need to be tempered by Children's Rights. Children are a privilege and a wondrous gift. Parents who abuse that privilege must be held accountable, even if that means losing their parental rights.

Children deserve no less.

We as a society deserve no less.

The very essence of human decency deserves no less.

Denial, incredulity, anger and sorrow are natural emotional reactions to learning that your child has been sexually abused, especially when the perpetrator is a loved and trusted member of your own family. You must not allow yourself to give in to those emotions. Your initial words and actions are of paramount importance to both the child's healing process and the court case that may well follow.

1. Believe the child! Children rarely lie about this kind of abuse.

2. Remove any sense of blame whatsoever from the child. Immediately reassure him/her that, "It was not your fault." It's natural to ask questions when confronted with this kind of disclosure, but queries such as, "Why didn't you tell me before?" or "Why didn't you call for me?" only provoke more fear and guilt in an already terrified child. Perpetrators control their victims with threats such as, "If you tell anyone, I will kill your mother"—or grand-mother or the family pets or whomever the child is most attached to.

3. Reassure the child that none of these things are going to happen. Praise the child for being so brave, and assure him/her that telling was the right thing to do. Let your child know how much you love him/her, and that you will do your very best to assure that this never happens again. Do not promise it will never happen again. No one can guarantee the outcome of any custody case, espe-cially when the accused is the biological father or mother. Family court entails investigations by so-

cial-service agencies, law enforcement and opposing counsels, among others, and no matter how much evidence you may believe you have, there is no guarantee you or your child will be believed.

4. DO NOT report the accusation of abuse yourself. Immediately take your child to a hospital or forensic specialist if there is physical evidence of abuse; unfortunately, over 70% of the time there isn't. Little bodies have almost magical healing powers, especially in the anus, and oral copulation does not leave any evidence on the body. You can, however, take the child to a qualified therapist and let him/her tell the professional what happened. The professional will then file a Suspected Child Abuse Report.

DIVORCE

If you are in the process of divorce at the time of your child's disclosure, expect more roadblocks than usual. Many social workers, health-care professionals and other investigators tend to be suspicious of any sexual-abuse allegations made during a divorce. They feel the non-offending parent is making up the allegations or coaching the child in order to gain an advantage in the custody case. Nothing could be further from the truth. In fact, the party that raises the child-sexual-abuse issue is more likely to lose custody altogether. Family Courts are not well-educated about child sexual abuse, and often accuse the protective parent of trying to alienate the child from the other parent.

This leaves you in a quandary over how to best protect your child while extricating you both from your legal union with the perpetrator. The fact is, the best you can do at this point is avoid making mistakes.

- As difficult as this situation is, remain calm.

- Focus on reassuring the child.

- Never confront the accused; you will not only be met with denial, you will be arming the perpetrator with information (of the child's disclosure) that can backfire against both you and the child.

- Find a trusted person to whom you can talk: a minister, rabbi, friend or, best of all, therapist. Do not be fooled; you will need therapy as much as your child will. Without a proper place to vent your hurt and anger, you risk decompensation, (the inability or desire to function), which will leave you unable to help your child.

REALITY

Regardless of the circumstances in your case, your life will never be the same after your child discloses sexual abuse. The pain and feelings of betrayal will always be with you and your child, even if the perpetrator is sent to jail. That does not mean that you will not eventually heal. Maybe you will use this devastating experience to help others who are going through the same trauma.

It is a sad fact that less than three percent of all incest cases nationwide are ever criminally prosecuted, according to the Department of Justice. Most District Attorneys will not put a child six years old or younger on the stand; they claim the youngsters do not make good witnesses. Nevertheless, some young children are extremely articulate, and can describe exactly what happened to them. Because they have no age-appropriate knowledge of sexual acts, they might, indeed, make excellent witnesses, if given the chance. At the very least, they are capable of speaking with the judge in chambers. Judges, however, rarely speak with child victims. The bottom line is, you have no control over these decisions.

You might be able to get criminal charges filed when the accused is a neighbor, grandfather, uncle, brother or baby-sitter—anyone who is at least once removed from the victim. Studies show that child sexual abuse perpetrators rarely have only one victim. Often, once a child victim discloses sexual abuse in a family, other family members come forward. They might rally to protect the innocent child—but this is not an absolute. In some families, the relatives rally around the accused perpetrator, and do everything they can to maintain the family secret.

Child sexual abuse is inappropriate, sexually oriented touching by an adult, at least five years older than the child. This involves masturbation, fondling, oral copulation and penetration. The definition can also be expanded to include showing the child pornography (often used to break down the child's inhibitions against sexual acts), inappropriate sexual acts in front of a child (masturbation, intercourse, oral copulation), not allowing the child privacy in the bathroom or bedroom, making lewd remarks or describing sexual acts, and any other actions of a sexual nature not age appropriate for a young child.

Incest is abuse by a blood relative, such as a father, mother, grandparent, uncle, aunt, sibling or cousin. Over the last few years, the incest definition has expanded to include stepparents, their children and other adults in extended families who have power and control over the child.

A word of caution to those who suspect their child has been sexually abused: beware of overzealous identification. A rash or redness in the genital area does not immediately equate to child sexual abuse. It is more than likely the result of poor hygiene on the part of the parent who is not experienced at cleaning little bottoms. Do not jump to the conclusion when a child says daddy/mommy touched my pee-pee. In fact, that could mean the parent was applying medication to an irritated genital area. Common sense must prevail here and one statement by the child should be listened to, but also investigated to the authenticity of what the child really means.

Child sexual abuse is one of the most damning accusations anyone can make against another individual. The public tends to believe the accused is "Guilty until proven innocent," and many innocent lives have been ruined as a result—especially in today's world, where divorced fathers are experiencing such things as potty training and diaper changes for the first time.

SIGNS AND SYMPTOMS

Although they have not yet been established as such within the legal system, the following chart includes the most prominent indicators of child sexual abuse. While each of these signs can occur for myriad reasons, five or more unexplained changes of more than one type should raise the sexual-abuse red flag. Remember: Do not question your child yourself. Take him or her to a professional.

UNEXPLAINED PERSONALITY CHANGES

1. Becomes introverted or secretive
2. Loses interest in grades, sports, hobbies or other pastimes
3. Becomes secretive about source or reason for gifts or money

UNEXPLAINED BEHAVIOR CHANGES

4. Cries constantly
5. Has "accidents" in undergarments or bedclothes after the child has been potty trained
6. Wears multiple layers of clothes in all kinds of weather
7. Is afraid of or refuses to use the bathroom
8. Is afraid of certain adult(s)

9. Is afraid to go to sleep, or has constant nightmares and night terrors

10. Sleeps excessively

11. Knows more about sex than other same-age children

12. Acts out sexually with other children beyond age-appropriate curiosity

13. Acts out sexually with adults

14. Acts out sexually with dolls or other toys

15. Masturbates excessively, or tries to force foreign objects into vagina or anus

16. Uses a vibrator or other sexual paraphernalia (older children)

UNEXPLAINED PHYSICAL CHANGES

17. Ongoing vaginal infections

18. Sexually transmitted disease

19. Vaginal scarring

20. Pre-adolescent broken or detached hymen

DECLARATION

21. Discloses sexual abuse

Notice that disclosure is the last way to learn that your child has been sexually abused. Children are often too frightened to disclose the abuse or to betray the secret. Pedophiles know how to scare children silent.

As noted, physical evidence of child sexual abuse is very rare, less than 30% of all cases. It certainly wouldn't appear from oral copulation, fondling, pornography or lewd descriptions. You must be alert, therefore, for such physical symptoms as difficulty walking, holding bowel movements, vaginal infections, difficulty urinating, fear of the bathroom, complaints of vaginal- or anus-area pain, blood or discharge on underwear. Sexual acting out with other children is a huge red flag, especially when the child is very young.

Many children who have been or are being sexually abused simply won't tell. Your child may display many of the above indicators, but deny that any such thing happened when questioned. He/she may be too afraid of the perpetrator, or feel ashamed or guilty. The child may have dissociated, or "spaced out" the abuse, or simply not be ready to talk about it.

As difficult and frustrating as it can be when you know your child has been sexually abused but he/she refuses to talk to social workers or law-enforcement officers, remember that child sexual abuse is traumatizing. Perpetrators often persuade their victims that they are at fault, are willing participants or are liars who no one will believe anyway. A child's entire basis of trust and safety is ripped away by sexual abuse; child sexual abuse and rape are the only crimes wherein the victim takes on the guilt of the perpetrator.

All you can do is wait until the child is ready to talk. Do not badger the child. Look for a children's therapist who is a child-sexual-abuse expert.

It may take months before the child actually discloses the abuse; children talk when they feel safe and can trust the adults around them.

DIVORCE

A child's silence is especially frustrating when the accused is the other parent and the allegation turns into a custody case, because without disclosure, the case can get bogged down to the point that it's next to impossible to protect the child. When a child won't disclose to the social worker, the case is usually deemed unsubstantiated and closed—even when the child's behavior is consistent with child sexual abuse, or, worse, when physical evidence actually does exist.

Unfortunately, indications you consider as "obvious" may be rejected by a pediatrician or other third-party as "inconclusive." Over the years, I have seen a three-year-old with a torn hymen and vaginal lesions that were deemed justified because she rode a tricycle. An enlarged anus on a four-year-old boy was dismissed as the result of bowel movements. Too many bubble baths explained away another child's consistent vaginal infections. A four-year-old's bruised and swollen penis theoretically came from a toilet seat falling on it. Improper hygiene somehow caused another child's chlamydia.

While some of these explanations seem plausible, and have been accepted by the court, the lingering question remains that the possibility of abuse was not considered. The fact that the allegations were never investigated as possible abuse issues is the problem. Most criminal acts are not straightforward. That is never so true as when a crime is committed against a child, who sometimes cannot even verbalize what happened. You must remain calm and focus on reassuring the child so he/she can feel safe and protected enough to talk to the right investigators at the right time.

Do not question your child!

THE SILENT FAMILY

Child sexual abuse is indeed the perfect crime, as it always comes down to the adult's word against the child's. Prosecutors may look for witnesses or corroborating evidence, but molesters do not perpetrate in front of other people. It's an intimate, one-on-one crime in which the perpetrator's credibility always outweighs the victim's.

Another complication results when family members, even those who have been victims themselves, are unwilling to testify. The scars child sexual abuse leaves never go away; decades later, victims are often unwilling or unable to hold perpetrators accountable.

"Incest does not happen in healthy families"—but it does divide allegiances in every family it touches. Denial is a major part of the equation; shame and embarrassment also rank very high. "We don't have those kinds of problems in our family" gives perpetrators a green light to commit further abuse, and permanently silence any victim who might have the courage to disclose. It is a slippery slope that will continue for generations until aggressively stopped.

Incest occurs in the best of families and the worst of families, although those in the upper socio-economic echelon stand less chance of detection by social-service agencies and law-enforcement officials. Children from these families seldom disclose, and are silenced immediately if they do. Sometimes, though, they can make great strides when they do speak up. Marilyn Van Der Bur Atler, Miss America 1968, is a perfect example.

Born into one of the most prominent families in Colorado, Marilyn was sexually molested by her father from age five to eighteen. She accidentally disclosed her secret when, unaware a reporter was in the audience, she gave a talk on child sexual abuse. Although traumatized by her disclosure being flashed across the media from coast to coast, Marilyn stood her ground and opened the floodgates for millions of survivors to talk about their own abuse. She turned her embarrassment into enlightenment, and took a step toward paving the way to remove the stigma and shame for victims of child sexual abuse: If it could happen to Miss America, it could happen to anyone. Survivors of child sexual abuse came out of the closet by the millions.

Many others, though, were apprehensive. They did not want to believe Marilyn could be an incest victim. Finally, her sister, an attorney in San Francisco, California, came forward and admitted that she, too, had been sexually abused by their father. Marilyn's statement to the press afterward was quite poignant:

"My God, if they won't believe me, who will believe the children?"

Non-offending parents of sexually abused children can be mothers, fathers, custodial grandparents or relatives, or even non-custodial parents or caretakers who become aware of the abuse of a family member—anyone, in fact, who believes the child has been sexually abused and wants to protect him or her from further abuse. Most are uneducated about the judicial system and the social-service agencies involved with child abuse, and expect the accused will be arrested, put in jail and never have contact with the child again.

If only it could be that uncomplicated!

CASE HISTORY

"Eric," the father of two little boys aged five and seven, shares custody with his former wife and their new stepfather. The boys spend almost every other weekend with their father. Overall, this was a relatively amicable divorce and custody agreement; Eric and his wife were on good enough terms to discuss the children's needs and make decisions together that would most benefit the boys.

One weekend, as Eric helped the boys bathe, he noticed they were both raw and inflamed in the anus area. In fact, the youngest child protested loudly when Eric attempted to help dry him. When he asked how they got hurt, the oldest boy immediately silenced his younger brother. "Shhh! We can't tell." Eric didn't question them any further. He just brushed it off as something that happens to kids, and the next several weekends went by without incident or physical signs. He did notice the boys were somewhat subdued—their usual exuberance just did not seem to be there—but he equated this with normal growing pains.

On a later visit, however, Eric's eldest son began using age-inappropriate language. When Eric questioned him on it, the child retorted, "Sam says I can say that. It's the game he plays with us." Horrified and disbelieving at the same time, Eric questioned his sons about their stepfather's "game." Although he knew virtually nothing about child sexual abuse, he understood oral copulation, fondling, child pornography and attempted sodomy.

Eric immediately contacted his ex-wife about their sons' disclosures. She was defensive and disbelieving, and accused him of trying to turn her children against her. She even called the boys liars, claiming they had made up this "nasty" stuff up about her husband.

Eric was taken aback by his ex-wife's adamant denial, and wondered if he was overreacting. Every time he relived his sons' disclosure and thought back to their swollen, inflamed anus areas, though, he felt sick. He knew something was going on. But what was the truth?

Not knowing to whom he could turn, Eric started to think he was losing his mind. Finally, he called Mothers Against Sexual Abuse.

Eric and I spoke for over two hours. While trying to give him the emotional support and validation he needed, I cautioned him to stay calm and not question the boys any further. I suggested several therapists who are child-sexual-abuse experts and worked with children. He made an appointment immediately; his amicable divorce-and-custody agreement made it easy for him to secretly take his children to a psychologist. He still was not sure his children had been sexually abused.

The boys were open and honest with the therapist, and repeated exactly what they had told their father about

Sam's "games." After the session, the therapist informed Eric that his sons had, indeed, been sexually abused, and that he was mandated by law to file a Suspected Child Abuse Report with the Department of Social Services. Eric was devastated.

A social worker visited the children at their mother's home. The boys denied everything and refused to speak further with her. The social worker deemed the case unsubstantiated and closed the file.

Meanwhile, World War Three had started between Eric, his former wife and the stepfather. Their nice, cooperative relationship disintegrated into blame, accusation, denial and acrimony. The mother stood firmly behind her new husband.

Eric hired a lawyer recommended by MASA, who explained the complexities of these kinds of cases, but was willing to file a motion for a change of custody. The boys were still seeing the therapist during Eric's visits, and the therapist was absolutely convinced the stepfather had sexually abused them.

Because this case covered a period of several years in family court, the following are just some of the highlights prior to the final resolution:

1. The judge flatly refused Eric's first request for a change of custody. The stepfather denied he had ever abused his stepchildren, and their mother supported him.

2. After the boys disclosed more information to their therapist, Social Services was contacted to investigate further. Again, questioned in their mother's and stepfather's home, the children recanted everything.

3. I suggested a background check on the stepfather to see if anyone else in his family had ever been sexually abused.

4. The background check produced a bonanza of information. In fact, he had been convicted and served prison-time for molesting his own two daughters.

5. Armed with this information, we felt sure we had enough for a "slam dunk."

6. The stepfather's criminal background was presented to the judge who, amazingly, ruled the evidence immaterial. He reasoned that Sam had been convicted of molesting girls, not boys, and besides, he must have been "cured" since he was now married to an adult woman.

7. Despite the setback, Eric relentlessly pursued the case for years. His ex-wife subsequently divorced Sam, and the boys petitioned the courts to live with their father. The petitions were granted. Today, they are both good students living happy lives.

The heartbreak, frustration, anger, despair and other emotions that were a part of this case for so many years could be a book in itself. Eric's critical mistake, although not his fault, was in confronting his ex-wife about the abuse. The accusation was immediately conveyed to the perpetrator, who had ample time to scare them silent.

The judge's complete ignorance about child sexual abuse, however, was heinous. Empirical research indicates that child molesters often cross-molest; availability is more of a key factor than gender or age preference.

GENERATIONAL CYCLE

The mother in this case was in deep denial, and chose—at least in the eyes of her sons, who have little to do with her now—to put her own happiness above the best interests of her children. As it turns out, she had good reason for her denial. She, too, had been a victim of incest by her father. She had never been able to deal with her own sexual abuse, so she could not possibly deal with her children's.

The mother's situation was far from unusual. At MASA, we have found that many non-offending parents of sexually abused children were incest and sexual-abuse victims themselves—over 85% of them, in fact. What makes victims gravitate to perpetrators? Psychological manuals classify this phenomenon as the generational cycle.

When a stone drops into a pond, it creates ripples that spread from the point of impact to the edges of the pond. The same thing happens in families: children learn from the adults, who learned from their parents, who learned from theirs, and so on. If a person's upbringing included physical, emotional, mental and/or sexual abuse, you can be fairly certain that person will raise his or her children the same way.

We are children for such a limited time, but the habits, attitudes and life patterns with which we are raised become ingrained during those short years. Without some sort of intervention or education toward a different way of life, a child will grow up to be the same kind of parent that raised him/her. Between the huge resistance families have to outside interference, and the reluctance social-service agencies and government have to getting involved, the family's ideology remains sacrosanct. Only the most egregious cases come to the attention of the family and juvenile courts.

FACTS ARE FACTS

Myth: Most molesters are strangers who prey on children in schoolyards and parks.

Fact: Over 85% of child-sexual-abuse incidents are committed by someone the child knows and trusts.

Myth: Sexual-abuse accusations are usually made to gain an advantage in a custody case or as part of a vendetta against the other parent.

Fact: An early 1990s American Bar Association report stated that only 2.9% of the child-sexual-abuse allegations raised in custody disputes were false, and that 85% of those were made in good faith.

The real "fact" of the matter is that most non-offending parents who make these accusations are horrified and trepid, not malicious or spiteful. Most perpetrators who take advantage of "trusting little children" are not sick, twisted strangers, but adult victims themselves, who wield the same power over their victims that was wielded over them, for the same reasons, in the same ways.

The only people who can break this unending cycle are the judges, social workers, police and other government officials who preside over the individual situations. And the only answers to helping them recognize and understand generational cycles of abuse are intervention, education and ever vigilance.

When the Founding Fathers introduced the concept of "innocent until proved guilty," they flew in the face of thousands of years of judicial tradition. In this country, no man, woman or child can be jailed on a whim or held indefinitely; we all have the right to answer specific charges at an arraignment. As a protection against governmental abuse of power and malicious prosecution, the burden of proof in any civil or criminal case must rest squarely on the accuser/prosecutor—and that proof must be sufficient to persuade a judge or jury of the respondent's/defendant's guilt beyond a reasonable doubt. Without question, being considered "innocent until proved guilty" is one of our most cherished rights.

How could the Founding Fathers have possibly envisioned the day it would be used to shield the most reprehensible perpetrators?

Incest and child sexual abuse are crimes committed in secret against victims so young they often cannot read or write, much less be considered credible witnesses in court. Certainly, a three-year-old's word holds little weight against the reputation and bemused, saddened, bewildered or irritated affect of the adult perpetrator. Most of the time, physical evidence is scant to none, or dismissed as having been caused by plausible childhood mishaps.

To compound the problem, most people have little or no comprehension of either the civil or criminal legal systems. They naively believe that justice will somehow prevail; after all, it always does on TV and in the movies.

The following is not a legal-advice primer, but an attempt to demystify the complex and often diabolically confounding systems with which you will have to deal when and if you make an accusation of incest or child sexual abuse, either for yourself, or on behalf of a child.

FAMILY COURT

Family court is where divorce cases are heard, where custody and visitation issues are resolved, alimony and child-support settlements are made and property is divided between divorcing partners.

Family court is not the appropriate court to hear issues of child sexual abuse. Nevertheless, many of the cases I've seen over the years have begun and ended in family court rather than be moved to dependency/juvenile courts because child-sexual-abuse allegations raised during divorce come under the authority of the family court handling the custody part of that divorce. Consequently, those allegations are automatically suspect by the judge, social workers, law enforcement, etc., as an attempt to gain advantage. Yet, if you were to find out your mate was sexually abusing your child, your first thought of recourse or defense would probably be divorce!

Thus, the protective partner is faced with the ultimate conundrum: you cannot let the child remain living with the abuser, yet you cannot get the child away from the abuser by divorcing him/her. Dealing with this dilemma at a time when emotions are running at their highest is the hardest thing a person can face.

UNDERSTANDING THE PHENOMENON

Most family-court cases do not involve issues of child abuse. Many couples deal with the terms of their divorce and the future of their children quite amicably. And while it is not my intention to minimize the trauma of divorce—a difficult, even horrifying situation for all parties—the "War of The Roses" type of marriage dissolution is, thankfully, still pretty rare.

What's more, the child-sexual-abuse issue is not commonly raised as the reason for the divorce. If it were, it might give the allegation more credence. No, the issue usually appears during the divorce proceedings, when the child victim finally feels safe enough to disclose to the non-offending parent.

The complications this phenomenon arouses are enormous. In the midst of trying to rearrange multiple lives and jockey who gets what, who pays what and who lives with whom, the child's disclosure amounts to a bombshell that came out of nowhere—especially since the non-offending parent is usually the one most in denial, not only about what is happening to the child, but often about what happened in his/her own childhood.

Thousands of non-offending parents have told me their first reaction to the disclosure of sexual abuse was that they simply did not believe the accusing child. Over the years, I have heard this response from enough non-offending parents to know it could not possibly be a ruse to gain advantage in a custody fight.

At this point in the proceedings, the non-offending parent has almost no allies, and usually knows very little about incest and child sexual abuse. If he/she confides in relatives and friends, they will often be too shocked and too much in denial themselves to be supportive. They will try to help find any other explanation for the child's disclosure—anything other than that the accused parent may have sexually abused his or her own child. So:

1.   The couple is going through a divorce;

2.   The child, removed from the abusive parent, discloses to   the non-offending parent,

3.   The non-offending parent's immediate reaction to the child is disbelief; or

4.   If the non-offending parent believes the accusation, the relatives' and friends' immediate reaction to the non-offending parent is disbelief.

Following such a sequence, it's almost reasonable that when the non-offending parent—angry, frightened and just plain distraught—brings up the issue during the divorce proceedings, the judge, attorneys and other court personnel also immediately respond with disbelief. The usual result is a highly contested custody dispute, because the accused parent never admits culpability. Without a confession, the case cannot come to the simple conclusion of awarding custody to the non-offending parent. No, because the Signs and Symptoms of child sexual abuse are not yet established within the legal system, this is the point at which things really can degenerate into "War of the Roses."

The attorney for the accused is bound by legal ethics to fight like a banshee for his or her client, leaving the burden of proof that any abuse actually occurred squarely in the accusing parent's lap. If the sexual abuse was reported in the usual way, the Department of Social Services will conduct an investigation. But when the social worker learns the parents are in a custody dispute, the accusation takes on a less-credible hue, and the subsequent investigation is often perfunctory. At that point, the judge usually orders a psychological evaluation on both parties to determine each parent's mental health and overall character. Here's what those reports often find:

The non-offending parent, horrified at the harm done to the child and the betrayal of his/her lifetime partner, appears distraught, frightened, anxious, angry and out of control.

The perpetrator, adept at putting up a front and manipulating everyone and everything around him/her, appears cool, personally injured by the accusation and in full control.

As they say in the movies, you do the math.

In the unlikely event the abuse is substantiated by the Department of Social Services, a custody decision could be made at this point—but it would require a great deal of presentable evidence. If there is enough evidence to raise a safety issue for the child, the judge may order supervised visitation for the accused parent until the investigation and psychological testing are concluded. Unfortunately, the supervisor is often a family member of the accused parent, and with most of them in complete denial that their relative could have committed such a heinous crime, supervision will be more lax than vigilant. A better solution for the safety of the child—or even just for the child's peace of mind—is a professional monitor, paid for by both parents.

NOT A GENDER ISSUE

While not all accused parents are fathers, many are. These fathers seek help from fathers' rights groups, which are very powerful. The accused father might even hire a Father's Rights attorney, who may embark on a mud-slinging campaign, or bury the non-offending mother and her attorney with paperwork, among other tactics. Remember, an attorney's job is to defend his/her client, not to amicably resolve the situation or even arrange the best outcome for the child.

Traditionally, fathers have more money than mothers, especially stay-at-home moms, who tend to be less assertive and, consequently, easier to manipulate and fool. They can afford to have the case continued over and over, running up the mother's legal fees, trauma and stress. These cases often cost tens of thousands of dollars.

At this point you may be asking, "What chance do I have?" The answer is, "More than you think."

First, do whatever is necessary to get calm and keep your emotions under control. Your anger, fear, frustration, hysteria and pain play right into the other party's hands. You cannot give up, for your sake and especially for your child, so plan on this being a long, slow, infuriating process, and take whatever steps you need to remain calm under the pressure. Find yourself the best support system possible.

Second, it almost goes without saying that you need a good attorney. Contact organizations that deal with child sexual abuse. A rape-crisis center may also know of attorneys that work with this issue. Remember, you are looking for an attorney who specializes in family law and has had some prior experience in dealing with cases involving child sexual abuse.

Third, bring your expectations down to earth. You are not going to get a "no contact" order for the accused parent, even if the abuse is substantiated. Reunification is a federal mandate. He or she will be ordered into some type of program such as one or more parenting, sex-offender, domestic-violence or anger-management class. Visits supervised by a professional monitor should be considered a win.

Do not let the courts see you as a parent who wishes to alienate your children from their other parent. Yes, that may be exactly what you want, but it is not likely to happen, and you could lose credibility with the courts.

Many times, these cases do not resolve in the non-offending parent's favor. If unsupervised visits are ordered the child may be sexually abused again, which, in my opinion, is nothing less than legalized child abuse. Although this may provide additional evidence of child sexual abuse, the price of further damage to the child is just too high. Until radical changes are made in the family-court system and judges, attorneys, social workers and other law-enforcement personnel undergo extensive education about the realities of child sexual abuse, the "innocent until proved guilty" law of the land will continue to shield perpetrators and further traumatize their victims.

DEPENDENCY/JUVENILE COURTS

Dependency courts, also known as juvenile courts, hear two kinds of cases: juvenile offenders and child abuse and/or neglect. Child-abuse cases that make it into juvenile court have already been substantiated by the Department of Social Services or law enforcement. Often, the children have already been removed from the home and taken into protective custody, placed in foster care or sent to live with a relative. The hearing for the offending parent(s) must take place within forty-eight hours of the children's removal from the home. Most juvenile courts are closed to the public due to confidentiality; only the parties involved in the case are allowed in the courtroom.

Juvenile courts are not infallible, but allegations of abuse are taken far more seriously. The professionals who investigated the case have already agreed that abuse has taken place, and give their report to the judge as part of the proceedings. The judge weighs the evidence—there is no jury—and a decision is made on the basis of ensuring the children's safety.

Remember, however: reunification is a federal mandate.

The judge will likely order a psychological examination for the offending parent, and a court-ordered program of parenting classes and any applicable alcohol-and-drug treatment, domestic violence, etc. Visitation with the children will also likely be ordered, often to take place at the Department of Social Services offices with a social worker as the supervisor. The Department of Social Services will monitor the offending parent's progress and court hearings will be scheduled, usually at ninety-day intervals. If the offending parent follows the court's orders, the judge will allow unsupervised visits with the children.

This process is designed to give the offending parent one year to complete the reunification program. A parent highly motivated to regain custody may complete the course in less time. Some parents simply refuse to comply with the court-ordered program, thus prompting a Termination of Parental Rights proceeding.

A child-sexual-abuse allegation is more likely to be directed to juvenile court if the parents are not in the process of divorce. Juvenile court has many advantages for the non-offending parent. Custody will likely stay with the non-offending parent as long as the offending parent is out of the home. The non-offending parent can get a court-appointed attorney if he or she cannot afford to hire one, and will receive more support from social workers and law enforcement, because the question of "false accusation" has been rendered moot.

CRIMINAL COURTS

Child-sexual-abuse cases rarely make it into the criminal courts for the myriad reasons previously discussed, but lack of evidence and the family's refusal to participate are the two most prevalent. The child's age is also a huge factor when seeking criminal prosecution.

The rules of evidence are given even greater weight in a criminal proceeding and, unlike family and juvenile/dependency courts, criminal trials have a jury. However, the District Attorney will not take the case to trial unless there is a good chance for a guilty verdict

The victim does not need an attorney; the District Attorney prosecutes the defendant. The victim becomes a witness for the state. None of this, though, means the victim's trauma and stress is not horrible. It is.

Do not expect the wheels of justice to turn quickly in a criminal court. Cases can drag on for many months, and the District Attorney may not be affable about responding to your inquiries. I have received hundreds of complaints from non-offending parents who are completely frustrated with the delays and lack of information from the District Attorney's office. Be patient. Remember, yours is just one case; the DA has hundreds to handle.

Do not expect a panacea. Many cases, especially those for first offenses, are plea-bargained. A "first offense" means the first time the perpetrator has been caught, not the first time he or she abused someone. What's more, juries are unpredictable; they may return a "not guilty" verdict. Still, for many victims, just having their day in court is empowering, whether or not they win. It can begin the healing process, and send a wake-up call to the accused about accountability. The next time this perpetrator is caught, that prior child-sexual-abuse charge may help sway the jury to a "guilty" verdict.

To the parent trying to protect his or her children, it must seem as if the American judicial system is completely failing the victims—and sometimes it is. Distraught parents faced with the choice of watching their child suffer further abuse or trying to find a safe haven have occasionally taken matters into their own hands and fled the jurisdiction of the courts into the underground. At the time they run, it must seem like the only viable option available.

Going underground is the very worst move a parent can make.

The accused parent will go into court ex parte (without the other parent or his/her attorney present) to seek full custody of the child. Once a judge learns that either parent in a custody case has fled the jurisdiction with the child, temporary custody is almost automatically granted to the other, and a bench warrant is issued for the fleeing parent. The FBI is notified—if you are in the midst of a court proceeding and you take the child out of jurisdiction without the court's permission, it's considered kidnapping, a serious felony. Suddenly, the non-offending parent has become a fugitive from the law and all judicial, social service and societal sympathy is extended to the non-fleeing parent—even when that parent has been formally charged with incest, an even more serious felony!

Because the protective parent has openly committed a felony, the full weight of the law will be vigorously applied, and the fleeing adult and child will be hunted. No such zeal will be applied to the parent accused of sexual abuse, because that crime, committed in secrecy, has not yet been proven in a court of law. The parent on the run, however, has committed his or her crime in plain sight of the law, and even if not convicted of kidnapping, is automatically guilty of contempt of court.

THE UNDERGROUND

The Underground is made up of well-meaning people who are willing to hide families who claim to be running from the abuse of the courts. At one time, the Underground was more organized, but even then it was neither foolproof nor safe. Most fleeing parents eventually get caught; some simply cannot run anymore and turn themselves in. However the end comes, the result is disastrous for both the protective parent, who is immediately taken into custody, and the child, who is turned over to the Department of Social Services prior to being returned to the person who holds temporary custody—the accused parent. All questions about that parent's fitness for custody are now rendered moot. The court will assume anyone who does not endanger the child by fleeing from the law must be a better parent than anyone who does. Nor will the court hear the abuse issues again—for similar reasons—so the non-offending parent's chances of ever regaining custody are very slim. Often, the non-offending parent will be lucky to get supervised visits with the child.

When emotions run high, it is hard to remember that judges and law-enforcement officials are just human beings, with normal reactions and foibles. When faced with a possible crime versus an obvious crime, they will lean toward the obvious; the obvious is, after all, a far more black-and-white issue and, consequently, affords an easier, more understandable and comfortable decision. I know too many non-offending parents, both mothers and fathers, who have fled with their children, gotten caught and subsequently not seen their children for years.

A CASE HISTORY

"Mary" and "John" had been married for five years before they had twin daughters, "Charlene" and "Angela." Mary thoroughly enjoyed being a stay-at-home mom. John, a busy insurance executive moving up the corporate ladder, nevertheless spent a great deal of time with his children. The couple had a beautiful home; life could not have been better. At the point our story begins, the four-year-old girls were actively testing their independence, deciding what they wanted to wear and enjoying pre-school.

One morning after she dropped the girls off at pre-school, Mary received an urgent call from the school's director, who asked her to come back. Thinking one of the girls had gotten hurt, Mary hurriedly returned. The director was waiting in her office with two of the pre-school's teachers.

The director told Mary that Angela had been caught in the bathroom trying to perform oral sex on one of the little boys. Both the teachers had witnessed this, and when they went to reprimand Angela, she cried, "But daddy lets me do it to him." Mary was stunned and horrified. All she could utter was, "There must be some mistake." The director explained that she was mandated by law to file a Suspected Child Abuse Report with the Department of Social Services, and that a social worker would contact her. She suggested Mary take the children home from school.

As soon as they got home, Mary began questioning her children, who told her about the games they played with daddy when she wasn't home. Their explicit descriptions left no doubt in her mind that something terrible was happening to the girls. Bereft, she began calling everyone she knew for advice, but her friends and family were as uneducated about child sexual abuse as she. John was out of the country on business; Mary had no way of contacting him. She decided there must be a mistake and that, somehow, this could all be explained.

Two social workers from the Department of Social Services arrived early the next morning. Mary had been up all night and was in a highly emotional state. The social workers spoke with her for a while, then asked to speak with the children alone. Mary woke them and led the social workers into the den for privacy. After about thirty minutes, the social workers informed Mary that the children seemed very credible, and that they would be turning their report in to law enforcement. John would have to leave the house and stay away from the children, or they would have to take the girls into protective custody. Sobbing and shaking, Mary told them that not only would John not be permitted to return home, but he would never see his children again.

When Mary finally reached John, all she could do was scream accusations. John denied everything, but agreed to stay away from the children.

Mary's next visitor was a female police officer who also talked to the children alone. She, too, told Mary the children had disclosed the sexual abuse, and that she would be turning the information over to the District Attorney's office. The officer also suggested that Mary take the girls to their pediatrician; however, the doctor found no physical signs of sexual abuse. Since the children were so young, it was their word against an adult's, and as the Signs and Symptoms of Abuse held no weight in court, the DA decided he did not have a prosecutable case.

For the next six months, Mary merely went through the motions of mothering the girls. John, true to his word, stayed away, but the couple regularly screamed at each other on the phone. The girls began wetting the bed, having screaming nightmares and crying for their father. With John out of the home Social Services closed the file, but since no charges were filed against him, Mary was in limbo about how she and the children would go on with their lives.

The day came when a process server showed up at Mary's door with a subpoena and a petition for divorce. John had hired a top divorce attorney who was also a well-known advocate for father's rights, and was suing for full custody. Mary became hysterical. Her parents stepped in and hired a lawyer for her.

At the court hearing, Mary's attorney argued a good case for the child-sexual-abuse allegations, but, of course, had no physical evidence. John's lawyer argued that his client had not seen his children in six months, and that Mary was coaching the children in order to gain custody. The judge refused to change custody, but ordered every-other-weekend visitations for John, and warned Mary of the penalties for false accusations. Mary and her family were stunned.

The visits went well at first. The children were delighted at being reunited with their father. He now had a girlfriend and they all got along, and did a lot of fun things together. Presents abounded. Mary began to relax a little; she enjoyed the short respites away from the girls. She told herself, "maybe this was some kind of phase and it will never happen again."

Sadly, it rarely works that way. Mary's case was no exception.

The children's nightmares and bedwetting returned. Charlene began masturbating and Angela kept trying to put foreign objects into her vagina. After Mary questioned them, the girls disclosed that daddy hurt their pee-pees, and was peeing in their mouths. Mary called her lawyer, who told her to make another Suspected Child Abuse Report to the Department of Social Services. The social workers came out to speak with the children again, but this time they would not disclose to the social workers and the report was deemed unsubstantiated.

FROM BAD TO WORSE

Although many Suspected Child Abuse Reports were filed over the next 2 ½ years, none were substantiated, and the numerous pediatricians who saw the girls were unable to confirm or deny child sexual abuse. Although they continued to disclose to Mary, the girls refused to talk to social workers or therapists. None of the court-ordered psychological evaluations validated the abuse or found either parent unfit, although Mary's showed emotional instability and "possible delusions." John continued to look like a choirboy.

Eventually, John's lawyer introduced Parental Alienation Syndrome to the case, a newly coined "malady" based on a scale designed by Dr. Richard Gardner, a known father's rights advocate, to measure parental alienation. While the scale had no scientific value, it was nevertheless adopted by attorneys representing parents accused of child sexual abuse.

The children's visits with their father became more traumatic. Both girls were literally screaming and kicking when put into their father's car. Mary became desperate. She had disobeyed the judge's demand that she stop bringing sexual-abuse allegations to the court, and was terrified that the judge would reverse custody to John.

All her lawyers' legal maneuvers had failed, and the fact that she was on her third attorney was used against her in court. The former attorneys had not been competent at presenting child-sexual-abuse cases, but the other side argued that she had fired them because they were not convinced any abuse had occurred. She would continue to go through attorneys, they claimed, until she found one who would agree with her wild accusations.

Another court hearing was coming up. The Order to Show Cause demanded that John receive sole custody of his children with supervised visits for Mary. Nothing had gone her way, or any way that would protect her children.

In desperation, Mary decided to take the girls and join a ragtag group of parents living on the lam. Shuffled from one family to another and one state to another, she quickly became exhausted and discouraged. She used pay telephone cards to call her parents, and cash to avoid a credit-card paper trail. But what if she or the children became ill or injured? They wouldn't even be able to use their medical insurance in the event of an emergency.

Finally, feeling on the brink of a breakdown, Mary walked into a police station in a different state and gave herself up. She was immediately arrested, charged with parental kidnapping, failure to obey a court order and a few other charges and jailed. The girls were taken into custody in that state until they could be returned to the sole custody of their father.

Fortunately, the FBI dropped the kidnapping charges, but Mary still had to justify why she had fled—and still had no more evidence than before. The judge found her in contempt of court and all ensuing charges, deemed her a flight risk and ordered supervised visitation.

Until something else happens, this case is over. Mary may have protected her children for a short while, but they are now in double jeopardy, ordered to live with their incestuous father and unable to obtain protection from their discredited mother.

What will happen to these children? How will they view the judicial system when they grow up? Victims of abuse tend to become either abusers or passive bystanders who allow the next generation to be abused. How can we stop this systemic cycle of child abuse?

Education! We must fight day-by-day, attorney-by-attorney, judge-by-judge, doctor-by-doctor and social worker-by-social worker, if necessary, to establish the Signs and Symptoms of Child Sexual Abuse as legitimate physical, or, at the very least, psychological evidence within the American legal system.

Social-service agencies have different names all across the country, but whether they're called Child Protective Services or Department of Social Services, their funding comes from the federal government and their mandate is the same: to protect children from child abuse and neglect. Their function is to investigate cases of child abuse and neglect and turn over their findings to the judge and other pertinent parties, such as attorneys and psychological evaluators. If the children are in foster care, social workers will oversee the foster homes as well as the needs of the foster children. It is an ominous task considering the enormous number of child abuse and neglect cases in this country. Some social workers have caseloads of eighty or more; as a group, they are overworked and underpaid.

More and more, social-service agencies across the country are coming under fire for failing to protect children. Too often, they do not take proper action when notified of ongoing abuse, especially if they have already visited the home many times. They may feel the report is just a case of "crying wolf." Sexual abuse leaves the least evidence and is consequently the most difficult to detect.

I know many wonderful, professional social workers in this vast system; some of them have become personal friends. However, even they admit that something is terribly wrong when so many cases—including most of the ones I have personally worked on— begin their downward spiral with the first investigation conducted by the social worker.

We have all heard the nightmare stories of children who get lost in the system, like the highly publicized case in Florida. Not only did they lose a child, but as of the completion of this writing, they still have not found her!

Florida is not the only state where child-protective agencies have gone awry. Illinois Social Services announced that they, too, have lost several children in their system. Is it unreasonable to imagine there are thousands of children missing across the country?

How could this happen? A number of factors contribute to the problem—overloaded, understaffed systems that create unreasonably heavy caseloads being the most glaring—but sometimes it comes down to just plain incompetence on the part of the social worker. In the Florida case, the social worker was not only incompetent, but dishonest—she outright lied about visiting the child monthly when, in fact, she had not visited in over a year.

In response to the public furor over this case, Governor Jeb Bush called for a full-scale investigation and social-services reform. As a result, Florida has set up a program to work with non-profit agencies that have the time, training and staff to help oversee the cases. We'll have to wait to see if this pilot program helps, but lowering each social worker's caseload and helping with the investigation process certainly seems like a reasonable start. The price of losing even one child is too high.

TOO MANY MISTAKES

Many non-offending parents have complained about social workers' unprofessional behavior, especially regarding the interviewing process. In some cases, the child barely talked with the social worker—and sometimes, that makes perfect sense. Suppose, for example, the accused perpetrator is male. How likely is the child to disclose to a male social worker? The child doesn't talk, the social worker has ten other people to see that day....

This puts the non-offending parent in a Catch-22 conundrum. The child has disclosed sexual abuse to the parent, sometimes other family members and perhaps the child's own therapist, but will not disclose to the social worker, a complete stranger. The social worker has almost no choice but to rule the abuse unfounded or, at the very least, unsubstantiated. Unsubstantiated does not mean it did not happen, but the term carries a lot of weight in court. If another social worker of the opposite gender talked to the child, perhaps he or she would disclose—but that would require reviewing each case individually before assigning a social worker, a concept that does not currently exist in any investigative system.

In another Catch-22, the social worker might decide the child is out of danger if the accused is out of the home, and close the case. That still leaves the child vulnerable during unmonitored visitation, and if the abuse occurs again, the non-offending parent could actually be charged with "Failure To Protect."

In April, 2003, I was called to testify before a Legislative Committee in South Carolina regarding their Social Service Agencies' failure to protect children. A six-year-old child had been beaten to death by the stepfather; the case was all over the newspapers and TV news.

This family had been reported to Social Services eleven times. The children had been removed from the home four times for on-going abuse. After the parents were ordered to attend some parenting classes, the children were returned to the home. Subsequent follow-up was minimal at best. While the stepfather was beating the six-year-old child again, a sibling dialed 911. The operator, however, was not astute, did not believe the child and actually hung up without notifying anyone to respond to the call.

The excuse for Social Services failing to protect this child and the other children in the home? Excessive caseloads. That excuse did not carry much credibility with the Legislative Committee.

NOW WHO'S IN DENIAL?

I testified as an expert by outlining the facts of several cases I had worked on across the country. I was exact in my presentation, and had prepared documentation for each assembly-person and senator. I was very flattered when one senator stated, "I think part of the solution to this problem is standing at the podium today. We should bring Ms. Reeves in to train the social workers."

An off-the-cuff remark, but many Social Service Agency representatives were in the audience, and I heard an audible gasp at the suggestion. I had trained teachers for many years in California, but I got the feeling I would not be welcomed by the agencies in South Carolina. They would prefer to administer their own programs in their own ways. Unfortunately, their programs and their ways are obviously part of the problem.

Let me be clear: I do not believe all agencies are corrupt nor all case workers deliberately callous. No one can deny they have extremely heavy caseloads; child abuse is out of control on every level.

I do believe, however, that high-risk parents should be a social worker's top priority. Neglecting the health and welfare of the children in these families is paramount to exacerbating and allowing the abuse. If that imposes on the time needed to investigate new accusations, then the answer is clear: we need to increase the Social Services budgets. Hiring and training enough people to handle the ever-increasing number of child-abuse cases is not an option—it is a necessity.

Many parents who felt they had been wronged by Social Services also testified, and one case stands out in my mind. A child entered the system after the mother had secured an outside, independent institution to help her troubled son. She was paying the institution through insurance and her own funds. When the institution proved unhelpful, she removed her son. The institution reported the removal to the Department of Social Services. They, in turn, removed the boy from his mother and took him into protective custody.

This was a thirteen-year-old boy who had never been in trouble with the law. He was simply having problems; his mother was doing what any mother would do, trying to help her son. During the next eleven months, the boy was placed in thirteen different foster homes. Finally, the mother's lawyer prevailed and he was reunited with his mother.

Approximately two months later, however, two social workers showed up at their house and claimed the boy had to be tested for the HIV virus that causes AIDS. They gave the mother no explanation as to why the test was necessary. Only after the mother's lawyer intervened with a threat to subpoena the records did she learn that the thirteenth foster father, who had just died of AIDS, had a history of sexually abusing children.

So much for proper foster-home screening.

Foster homes and child sexual abuse are entirely different issues, but they are managed by the same Social Services Agencies, and the lapses in judgment about ensuring the best interests of the children are the same. Yet, these agencies and their employees are almost always immune from prosecution or lawsuits unless it can be proved a social worker deliberately endangered a child. Incompetence may be destructive, but it is not criminal. Most times, the social worker will not even face a reprimand.

THE CARNAGE IS ON US

We as taxpayers pay the bill for Social Service Agencies' errors. Healthcare, incarceration, abuser-rehabilitation, increased crime and sanctioning an attitude of victimization and entitlement are all part of the equation. Denial and minimization are luxuries we cannot afford to accept. Not only is the system not working, it is in crisis. It needs to be overhauled.

If you feel your case has been wrongly handled by a social-service agency, do not be afraid to speak out. Contact your legislators about hearings such as the ones held in South Carolina. Local town meetings that allow many people to testify may also expose errors and injustices.

Reporting your social worker to a supervisor may also be an option, but it must be done in the most diplomatic manner, giving the social worker the benefit of the doubt. Document the problems and present them to the supervisor in a non-accusatory fashion. Keep in mind the evidentiary requirements of proving child sexual abuse. Even the best investigative social worker cannot substantiate sexual abuse without either evidence or the child's disclosure.

GUARDIAN-AD-LITEMS

One definite source of remedy is the Guardian-ad-Litem program. Guardian-ad-Litems are court-appointed special advocates for children who have suffered abuse or neglect by their biological families, usually the parents. Some Guardians are attorneys, but many are not; they are volunteers with a deep commitment to the health and safety of children. Most states have Guardians, and most Guardians work in dependency or juvenile courts. They are the voice in court dedicated to the protection and needs of the child victim.

While the Guardian does not replace the Department of Social Services social worker, he or she usually has a much closer relationship with the child. The Guardian visits frequently, and understands the child's view of his/her situation. The Guardian also interviews all persons directly involved in the child's life, prepares a report for the judge regarding the best interests of the child, and presents that report in court.

Of course, no system is foolproof. Some states have such low Guardian qualifications that their programs are really just another layer of people who can do as much harm as good. For the most part, however, Guardian-ad-Litems are a true beacon of hope and comfort in most social-service quagmires. Check with your state or county offices for information on finding or becoming a Guardian.

In contested child-custody cases, the judge commonly orders a psychological evaluation of both parents. This is good practice, in theory. The judge wants to know as much as possible about each parent in order to render a judgment in the best interests of the child. The court provides a list of approved psychological evaluators, and the chosen psychologist interviews all parties and administers the Minnesota Multiphasic Personality Inventory, or MMPI, a widely used and accepted psychological-profile test. The evaluator may administer other tests as well, and conduct extensive interviews with all parties. The evaluator then presents his/her findings to the court in a report that carries a great deal of weight as to who will gain custody of the minor child.

There are two problems with these tests: 1) an individual's answers can vary widely from day-to-day or even hour-to-hour, depending on his or her state of mind and emotional security at the time the test is administered, and 2) the evaluator may have an undisclosed agenda.

The first problem is probably the easiest to understand. When the non-offending parent meets with the evaluator, he or she is usually still reeling from discovering the child has been sexually abused. Consequently, the tests will often indicate that the parent is over-emotional, anxious, frustrated and angry. Who wouldn't be?

Unfortunately, the evaluator may then conclude that, based on the tests, the parent is unstable and has emotional problems. In the meantime, the accused looks calm and collected. No test can reveal guilt or innocence, or whether or not an adult is a pedophile.

HIRED GUNS?

Most court-appointed psychological evaluators are ethical and honest, but, as in any situation that involves power, authority and accountability, some are not. In Los Angeles County, for example, several evaluators are known to be fathers' rights advocates. Defense attorneys know very well who will likely give the most favorable evaluation for their clients. Plaintiff attorneys, on the other hand, who do not necessarily deal with child-sexual-abuse cases on a regular basis, may not share that knowledge. If the plaintiff's attorney is unaware of these individuals' bias, the result can be disastrous for the protective parent. Once an evaluation has been presented to the judge, it becomes part of the court record.

Sometimes, an evaluation is so egregious to the non-offending mother that she hires an outside rebuttal evaluation. However, the judge is not obligated to accept the rebuttal because the new evaluator is seldom on the panel of approved and court-appointed evaluators. Hence, the initial damaging report remains permanently on the record.

Why not simply seek out another court-appointed evaluator? Because no judge will allow a party to the action or his/her attorney to "shop" the list just because the evaluation is derogatory. Which is fair enough — except when it isn't.

NOT EVEN SUBTLE

One particular Los Angeles County evaluator has never, to my knowledge, written a favorable report for a mother who suspects the father of child sexual abuse. A few years ago, I reviewed the psychological evaluations of seven mothers who were examined by this evaluator. They were almost identical—only the names had been changed. And every one of these mothers lost custody of their children to the father accused of sexually abusing them.

At a recent court hearing, I was astonished at the testimony of another case's psychological evaluator. He had interviewed me several months earlier on behalf of the non-offending mother, but had severely misquoted me in the ensuing report, as well as a number of other professionals advocating for the mother. The mother had lost custody of her daughter to the father whose son, the girl's stepbrother, had sexually abused her. The sexual abuse had been substantiated and the brother was not supposed to be alone with the child.

However, unsubstantiated allegations had also been made against the father, so the court had ordered supervised visitation. The father's current wife was named as supervisor, and the father was given custody of the minor child.

The evaluator rendered a completely false and biased testimony in favor of the father and demonized the mother. The father had just separated from his new wife, on whom he had cheated with yet another woman in an ongoing affair. That wife attended the hearing to testify about the father's relapse into alcohol and drugs, and stated that on the way to the court, he had tried to run her off the road with his car. Her sister, a passenger in the car, corroborated the incident.

The evaluator, on the other hand, testified that the father was in no way a danger to his child or anyone else. He called the return to alcohol and drugs "just a little relapse," ignoring the man's long history of severe alcohol and drug abuse. The father denied the affair despite overwhelming evidence to the contrary, so the evaluator claimed it likely never happened, and asserted that the MMPI administered to the father over eight months earlier was still relevant to the father's emotional and mental stability. The evaluator even went so far as to say that as a functioning and healthy individual, the father needed no therapy.

Although it was brought out in court that the father had paid the evaluator $1,500.00 for his day in court, the judge leaned on every word, and showed indications of non-verbal agreement with the testimony. In an interesting side-bar, however, when the judge learned he might be involved in a civil suit filed by the non-offending mother, he immediately recused himself. The case was continued until assigned to another judge, and the little girl's life left in limbo, her fate to be decided at some undisclosed future date.

KNOWLEDGE IS POWER

Even if you have lost custody of your child, you can take steps to remedy the damage of a dishonest or unethical psychological evaluator. Get a rebuttal evaluation by another psychologist; even if the judge rejects it, it will still be entered into the court record. Make sure you choose an attorney who knows the good and bad evaluators, and have him or her demand that the raw materials of the evaluation be turned over to another evaluator for consideration. Of course, pre-empting an unethical evaluator before testing is far more prudent than trying to undo the damage afterwards.

Do not make the mistake of considering the evaluator your friend. They may be friendly, but that is, after all, their stock-in-trade. They are there to do a job, so be careful to not make negative comments about your spouse; you do not want to give even the slightest indication that you are an alienator. Be scrupulously honest on the MMPI—the test is built to discern lying and/or equivocating. Try to be as objective and honest about yourself as you can.

As I mentioned above, almost every evaluation I have ever read portrays the non-offending parent as anxious, angry and stressed, which seems beyond reasonable to me. To combat this result, try to go into the evaluation as calmly as possible. Put your frustration and anger aside, and concentrate on your feelings of protection and love for your child. Try to answer the questions as you would have before you learned about the child sexual abuse. While not a miracle remedy, the effort itself may put you into a better frame of mind when you take the test.

I cannot emphasize this enough: you must have your own therapist and support system. On a crisis-level scale of one to ten, contested-custody cases that involve child-sexual-abuse allegations rate a solid eleven.

Seek out support groups for non-offending parents. Rape-crisis centers often have lists of these groups. Your therapist knows some as well, or may be treating other non-offending parents and offer group therapy. Ask your attorney if he knows about other parents facing this crisis, and if he/she would ask if they would be willing to speak with you.

Attend other family-court cases. (You will not be able to attend juvenile court hearings). You will find that your case is not that rare, and it may give you an opportunity to meet the non-offending parent whose case is being heard.

Check the Internet for child advocates and other parents who are trying to protect children. You must have a sounding board that is knowledgeable and understanding of these very complicated cases. Support and camaraderie can alleviate some of the trauma and challenges to your self-esteem, and help you realize you are not alone, or crazy, or vindictive, or an alienator—no matter what any test or evaluator may claim.

*Syn•drome: a number of symptoms occur-
ring together and characterizing a specific
disease or condition; any set of character-
istics regarded as identifying a certain
type condition. (New World College Dictionary, Fourth Edition)*

Fact: A syndrome is a psychological or physical
illness recognized in medical and scientific
journals.

Fact: Parental alienation syndrome is not recognized in either the Diagnostic & Statistical
Manual IV or the International Classifica-
tion of Disease & Disorders, the "bible" for
the mental-health professions.

Fact: Without benefit of scientific credibility, peer
review or even traditional publishing credence, parental alienation syndrome is used
in family and dependency courts throughout the country to discredit mothers and return custody of their children to husbands
who are accused of sexually abusing those
children.

What?

Dr. Richard Gardner, a Columbia University
professor of clinical psychiatry who died by his
own hand May 25, 2003, self-published several
books depicting his contempt for child-protection
agencies and any professional dedicated to protecting children from sexual abuse. Gardner made
it his crusade to discredit all children's advocates.
In one book, he claimed that working in the child-
sexual-abuse field was a way for professionals to

gratify their own sexual perversions and that, "there is a little bit of pedophilia in each of us."

In answer, a doctor friend of mine said, "Anytime a doctor uses his education and training to confuse and mystify the public, you can be assured his message has little, if any, credibility."

Despite all of that, many defense attorneys immediately developed an almost cult-like faith in Richard Gardner. At last they had something that sounded authoritative to use against what they believed to be alienators and false accusers. And, as incredible as it sounds, it worked. Mothers across the country were diagnosed with this non-existent syndrome. Mothers—Richard Gardner never applied the term "Alienator" to a father, accused or otherwise, who was trying to gain custody of his children. When a child disclosed sexual abuse by the father and the mother dared to take appropriate steps in court to protect that child, she was immediately identified as an alienator. Thousands of mothers were accused of making up the allegations and coaching their children to gain a custodial advantage. One doctor, after witnessing a particularly brutal hearing that accused the mother of parental alienation syndrome, said to me, "If coaching a child is so easy, why is it so difficult to coach one to use the potty?"

How poignant. How true. How absurd to think anyone can successfully coach a child less than five years old to tell the same story or describe the same incident, again and again, with no variation in the telling. Most adults could not master that feat.

A TINY SPECK OF TRUTH

Of course, it is true that some selfish parents will use their children as bullets in the gun aimed at the other parent, whether abuse is alleged or not. The damage to these children is heartrending and often irreparable.

But those parents are in the minority. As reiterated in previous chapters, most non-offending mothers and fathers lapse into complete denial when their children disclose sexual abuse. Alienating the children from their spouse—the person they loved and trusted, the person they married and with whom they expected to spend the rest of their life—is the farthest thing from their minds. Yet, Gardner has a huge following of "Gardnerites," as many child advocates in the legal and psychological professions call them. It might help to look at what those Gardnerites believe.

In l991, Gardner self-published Sex Abuse Hysteria: "Salem Witch Trials Revisited." In it, he proffered a "Sexual Abuse Legitimacy Scale," or SAL, that would supposedly separate real allegations of child sexual abuse from false one by registering a series of criteria in each case. In 1998, Jon Conte, Ph.D., an expert in the field of child sexual abuse wrote: "Probably the most unscientific piece of garbage I've seen in the field in all my time. To base social policy on something as flimsy as this is exceedingly dangerous."

Needless to say, this scale identified neither real nor falsely accused abusers. The scientific community, including child-sexual-abuse experts, simply could not accept it. So how did Gardner embed himself and his theory syndrome so deeply into our court systems?

To start, we cannot rule out gender bias. Some judges are simply very patriarchal. Child sexual abuse is a nasty issue, and denial is far more comfortable than believing that this nicely dressed man, respectable in every other area of society, could possibly violate a child in such a heinous manner. Parental Alienation Syndrome certainly sounds authentic and scientific, and Dr. Gardner's credentials sound impeccable—until you read his books.

Then again, most judges have not read any of Gardner's writings. They merely find it easier to accept the defense attorney's rhetoric about him than to believe the accused is really an incestuous father. When the psychological evaluation, done by a psychologist with his own agenda, also portrays the mother as an alienator, the judge feels justified in accepting the mother as the real culprit.

These are very complicated cases, and their dynamics require thorough, delicate legal and psychological scrutiny. The idea of basing a decision that affects the lives and safety of children on unfounded theory shrouded in psycho-babble is despicable.

COMBATING PARENTAL ALIENATION SYNDROME

If you have been accused of parental alienation syndrome, do your research. If your attorney is not educated about Richard Gardner, educate him/her. Read Gardner's books and research the trials in which he testified as an expert witness. Have your lawyer prepare the negative information about Gardner—there is plenty of it available—and present it to the judge.

After several derogatory articles about Richard Gardner appeared in the newspapers, a defense attorney tried to use Gardner's theories in a Los Angeles County case. The presiding judge ruled that parental alienation syndrome would no longer be allowed as a defense in contested-custody cases when there are allegations of child sexual abuse. Nevertheless, many other judges continued to automatically view mothers as alienators. Fortunately, proactive child advocates sat in on many of those cases, and consequently were able to discover and expose those " Gardnerite" judges.

Time has also exposed the flaws in Gardner's theories, and attorney education has reduced some of the damage he afflicted with his influence over judges' decisions. As the courts become better educated and the number of protective advocates increases, Richard Gardner's influence will continue to fade. After all, it is difficult to argue with statistics provided by the United States Department of Justice: one out of three girls and one out of four boys will be sexually violated one or more times before they reach age eighteen.

I received hundreds of emails once the word was out that Gardner had taken his own life. Not one expressed sympathy at his passing, but a number did compare the pain and suffering he caused to the devastation Hitler wrought. I hate the idea of anyone committing suicide, but I believe he hurt more children and non-offending parents than any other single American in the history of the country. We can only hope his phony parental alienation syndrome died with him.

FEMALES

Female child-sexual-abuse survivors are quite different from male survivors. Both genders, however, may show the same debilitating behavior patterns throughout their lives: alcohol and drug abuse, promiscuity, difficulty with adult relation-ships, lack of direction, a learned feeling of help-lessness and sometimes crossing the line and be-coming perpetrators themselves. But while males are more likely to minimize the impact of their abuse, females' lives can be in a decline for years until they deal with those issues.

On the other hand, some women, like Oprah Winfrey, become very high achievers. Probably the country's most famous child-sexual-abuse survivor, Oprah had the courage to disclose on national television, opening the floodgates for survivors everywhere to overcome their shame and deal with the trauma of their abuse. If it could happen to Oprah, it could happen to anyone. Through her many shows on this disturbing issue, she has educated audiences around the world and become a heroine to millions of adult survivors.

Other high-achieving female survivors, who keep their abuse a secret and do not deal with the inherent emotional issues, often find themselves almost shut down in later life. The burden is just too great not to share. These women have intense trust issues. They maintain a lonely vigil to protect their emotions to the exclusion of living a full and happy life.

For adult female survivors, the first step in healing is telling, yet telling is also one of the most difficult steps. Whether the abuse was committed by a family member or a neighbor, teacher, family friend, etc., talking about it or attributing some of their life's problems to the child sexual abuse they suffered as children is very difficult.

One survivor told me it was hard to mourn the loss of her childhood without beating herself up for what she felt was her own culpability in aiding and abetting her abuser. Again: child sexual abuse and rape are the only crimes where the victim so often takes on the guilt of the perpetrator. Perpetrators are adept at thoroughly convincing their victims that they are willing, active participants.

This is where reality meets fantasy. The child is never, ever a willing participant and should never be considered a willing participant in any fashion. It is always the responsibility of the adult to have the moral and ethical boundaries to not violate a child. Child sexual abuse may be considered a matter of power and control over children from a psychologist's viewpoint, but it manifests itself in a sexual nature, and as such, needs to be recognized as a sex crime.

Children who are abused before age six often have no frame of reference as to what is normal. Many survivors have told me they thought what happened to them happened to all children. Accepting that a most-trusted adult violated them and left them with such confusing emotions is painfully difficult for survivors of early childhood sexual abuse, especially in cases of incest.

"SUSIE'S" STORY

I agreed to an intervention for "Susie," a survivor who had been molested by both her uncle and godfather. At nineteen, she was experiencing flashbacks of her abuse and having difficulty with daily functioning. Her sadness and depression overshadowed all the joy in her life.

Susie and her mother called all the members of their large family and set the intervention for a Saturday night. My job as mediator and counselor was to see that everyone had a chance to present their point of view, and that Susie found some kind of suitable resolution that would help her recovery.

This was a very controlled and intense environment. First, Susie disclosed the child sexual abuse she had endured, and named the perpetrators, both of whom were present at the meeting. The perpetrators and some other family members objected, but Susie was definitely going to have her say, and she did.

Amazingly, after Susie poured out her story, the two men admitted their guilt. They both apologized and asked for forgiveness. The uncle said if he had ever thought it would hurt his niece so much, he never would have committed such an act. I did not believe that for one minute. The accused uncle had become a therapist, and was well aware of the damage he had caused. His remorse and concern seemed genuine, however, which was the entire point of the intervention. Susie's godfather, on the other hand, only admitted his involvement in the abuse after the uncle had admitted his part.

The intervention produced some healing within the family. At the end of the evening, there were tears, healthy hugging and a promise to pay for any therapy Susie needed.

I have since learned that the uncle and godfather were true to their word about paying for Susie's therapy, but the family was and is still very divided as to how they felt about the seriousness of the abuse she experienced. Interestingly, her grandmother was the one who minimized it the most. She said it had happened to her as a child and she had just "gotten over it." The uncle's fiancé disclosed that she, too, had been a victim of child sexual abuse, and also tried to minimize any trauma it had caused her. Other family members blamed Susie, and remain angry with her and her mother to this day, minimizing her pain and trying to invalidate the harm done to this young woman.

No question about it, incest splits the family!

Susie had the courage to stop what was likely a generational cycle in her family. It is not unreasonable to assume that her abusers might also have been incest victims, although nothing of that nature was disclosed. I had hoped the family would convey a zero tolerance for future sexual abuse of the youngsters in their family. Whether that will be accomplished remains to be seen. Susie's courage and her mother's support cannot be underestimated. At least the issue has been raised and validated in this family. If the family as a whole finds the courage to address child sexual abuse as a serious problem and do something about it, healing can occur.

RECOVERING AND MOVING ON

The most encouraging thing about adults who were sexually abused as children is their amazing capacity to recover and move on through intervention and therapy. Of course, without support, it is not likely to happen, because the trauma and insidiousness of this kind of abuse must be addressed to be resolved.

First and foremost, survivors must believe the abuse was not their fault. They must also realize that recovery is no panacea, and may take years longer for some than for others. Certainly the severity of the abuse is a factor, but the individual's personality, emotional make-up, learned coping skills and even genetic coding all play a part in the extent of the trauma and the speed of recovery. One survivor might have been more traumatized by fondling than another who experienced all-out rape, but that in no way minimizes either crime. No aspect of child sexual abuse can or should ever be minimized.

An individual's reaction will help dictate the best healing method. Someone who grew up in a loving family and was sexually abused by an outsider may be able to draw on his or her family's stability and love for healing. On the opposite end of that spectrum, someone who disclosed incest and received no validation or support from family members will likely be far more traumatized.

Over the years, I have had the privilege and honor to speak with thousands of child-sexual-abuse survivors in every phase of their recovery. Many who contact MASA are just beginning their journeys. One of the first things I tell them is that they can take control of their own lives. Yes, the perpetrator has robbed them of a childhood that cannot be replaced, but they have control over their future and they cannot allow their abuser to take one second of that future. Survivors are in control of their own destinies.

These words are like magic. So many women have told me they never thought of it that way. It is very empowering for a child-sexual-abuse survivor to realize she has control of her own life, the very thing her abuser stripped from her as a little child.

Some survivors just do not make it. I once worked with "Janet," a 32-year-old woman who was struggling with the abuse she had suffered as a child. Janet's life was out of control. She had run the circuit of abuse symptoms from prostitution to multiple abortions to alcohol and drug dependency.

When she finally met a supportive and wonderful man who wanted to marry her, she came to MASA for help out of her cycle of despair. I found her a child-sexual-abuse expert and she immediately started therapy. Sadly, it was too little, too late; Janet committed suicide one weekend when I happened to be out of town. Her messages were an ominous reminder of the life-and-death ramifications of this odious crime.

ADULT MALE SURVIVORS

Male survivors are definitely different from females. If the abuse occurred pre- or during adolescence, they often do not look at it as real abuse. A pre-teen boy abused by a baby-sitter or older woman may think of it is a great experience, and minimize any derogatory effects. One adult male survivor told me that at the time, he thought it was the greatest thing to tell his friends about.

It is certainly easier to justify male child sexual abuse, especially with older female abusers. Boys cannot become pregnant, and do not have the same societal expectations of being a virgin as females do. But from a parental point-of-view, it looks quite different. Would you want your 10- or 11- or 12-year-old son to have his first sexual experience with someone far older? Do you think he could possibly be emotionally mature enough to handle such a heady experience and the potential emotional, psychological and physical consequences? Wouldn't you prefer he have his first experience with a same-age mate of his choice at a more appropriate time of his life?

One of the very first cases I handled through MASA concerned a woman who had molested several young boys. Mary Lee Lynn lured boys age fourteen and under to her home, plied them with alcohol and engaged them in sexual acts, including oral copulation.

As spokesperson for the victim's families, I was sickened by the media exposure that profiled and minimized the abuse, portraying it as a right of passage for these young boys. Jokes abounded, denigrating the seriousness of the crime. At that time, California's statutory-rape age was sixteen for girls and fourteen for boys.

The mother of one of Lynn's younger victims authored the California Gender Bill. Supported by MASA, the bill established a uniform statutory-rape age of sixteen for both males and females. It passed unanimously.

So what happened to Mary Lee Lynn? She was convicted and sentenced to probation. If a man had been convicted of sexually abusing multiple victims, he would probably have gone to jail. Americans are just not ready to face the reality that females also commit child sexual abuse.

Too Young AND INNOCENT

Minimizing the damage inflicted on teen boys who have been sexually abused is a very grave error. It is not every teen-age boy's dream—it is abuse, pure and simple, and should not be painted as anything else. These too-young victims are robbed of their childhood and face the same trauma as female victims of child sexual abuse.

Same-sex molesters are lethal to young and teenaged boys who have no understanding of their own sexuality. The confusion it causes can last the rest of their lives. Survivors have told me they thought they were gay; they didn't know if they could have a sexual relationship with a woman; the abuse took away their basic understanding of their own sexuality. The same problems females face, such as alcohol and drug abuse, promiscuity, relationship failures, also apply to male survivors in varying degrees.

Ego is a huge part of the male survivor's cover-up. Society still burdens boys with their macho images. Between our societal perspective and the male tendency to minimize their own experiences, it is very difficult to determine the numbers of adult males who were sexually abused as children.

The good news is that more and more men are finding the courage to come forward, paving the way for other male survivors to shed the shame and secrecy and talk about what happened to them. Support groups for male survivors are forming all across the country as they realize there is absolutely no shame in being an adult survivor of child sexual abuse. The abuse was no more their fault than it was for female adult survivors.

Healing and moving on is the best revenge, and talking about it is still the best way to start that healing process. The younger any survivor can begin dealing with the abuse he suffered, the longer he will have to lead a full, happy life. Healing may be a lifetime journey, but it does not have to be all sadness and trauma.

Helping others is also a wonderful catalyst for your own healing. I know many male survivors who work with younger survivors through mentoring programs, Alcoholics Anonymous and other outreach programs. Remember, the perpetrators of this vile crime took what you had no control over—your childhood. The rest of your life is up to you.

WHO MOLESTS CHILDREN?

For many years, most people's impression of a child molester was a man in an over-sized raincoat that flashed children in the school-yard. While such exhibitionists still exist, research and expanded knowledge have revealed that child molesters are found in all shapes, sizes, professions, religious affiliations, parents, extended family members and even clergy.

It is impossible to recognize a "pedophile/child molester." He is most likely the person you would least suspect: the dedicated soccer coach so supportive of the youngsters under his supervision. The devoted baby-sitter who seems so trustworthy. A longstanding family friend who has been there for christenings and holidays and other important family events. The dear, caring friend you can always count on for a break when life becomes engulfing. The harmless relative that the family jokingly refers to as a "dirty old man"—don't be so sure about the harmless part.

The examples go on and on. Statistics show that over 85% of child sexual abuse is committed by someone the child knows and trusts. Most of us think our children are immune from suffering this kind of abuse. We would never let "anybody like that" around our children.

Oh, but child molesters are very good at what they do. They scare their victims silent or indoctrinate them to believe they are party to the "games" of their own violation. Children are vulnerable to every word uttered by an adult, and threats are taken in the most literal sense. No family, and certainly no child could possibly be immune to such predators.

THE PEDOPHILE

Not all child molesters are pedophiles. According to Webster's New World College Dictionary, Fourth edition, pedophilia is "an abnormal condition in which an adult has a sexual desire for children." Pretty straightforward, but what about adults who sexually molest children, but seem to have normal, happy relationships with other adults, such as a wife or girlfriend?

Perhaps the answer lies in the word "molest," defined by the same dictionary as "interfere, annoy, meddle with so as to trouble or harm, or with intent to cause harm. To make improper advances to; especially of a sexual nature; to assault or attack."

No, definitions really tell us very little about the profile of an adult who crosses the boundaries of everything decent and sexually violates a child. But years of experience and research helps shed some light on these disturbed individuals.

THE FIXATED PEDOPHILE

Without being overly clinical, the fixated pedophile is an adult who likely would never have a relationship with an adult partner or same-age mate. He is only attracted to children, and may be fixated on a particular age and gender. Beyond those criteria, he is particularly fixated on the child's availability. In other words, while he may have a preference, he will settle for any child he can get to, period.

The fixated pedophile is the type most likely to physically harm or kill his victims. Their psychological diagnoses include bi-polar disorder, borderline-personality disorder, schizophrenia, psychotic and any number of other mental illnesses. He may have strong anti-social tendencies and be a loner, or he may have a career working with children.

Fixated pedophile predators are part of the 15% of perpetrators who are likely to not know or be known by their victims. They prey on children from shadows, sidewalks, open malls and car windows. If we only had to worry about these criminals who target children unknown to their families, all child sexual abuse would be regarded as the terrible crime it is. Beyond these few facts, though, we have no real profile for the fixated pedophile.

How can we possibly protect our children against such monsters if we cannot even identify them? Education, first, last and always. Talking to your children about sex may be uncomfortable, but it certainly won't be as uncomfortable as sobbing over his or her mangled body and regretting the conversations you didn't have. Straight talk about sex is a necessary part of any child's education in today's world. You wouldn't think of sending your child out in below-zero weather without a warm coat; sending your child out in a predatory world without a shield of knowledge is just as negligent.

THE REGRESSED PEDOPHILE

The regressed pedophile, by far the most common type, is likely to be an incestuous father, uncle or other adult the child knows and trusts. These predators are almost impossible to recognize until the abuse is disclosed. They usually have a wife, girlfriend or significant other of the opposite sex, and are functioning as a decent and respectable member of the community.

Men with such a dark side may sexually abuse children at times of high stress. Divorcing fathers suffering from low self-esteem, for example, may turn to their daughters for comfort and acceptance, using them as catalysts to satisfy their own inadequacies. They have no grasp of their own selfishness, moral turpitude and blatant disregard for their child's welfare. They have no conscience about exploiting a child already suffering the effects of divorce.

Regressed pedophiles are of a garden variety. Experts call regressed pedophilia a crime of power and control that is not really about sex at all. I strongly reiterate: when power and control manifests itself sexually, it is a sexual crime. Whatever we label the abuser, the devastation to the victim sentences him or her to a lifetime of healing and recovery.

Parents and other relatives can often identify in hindsight what now seems like blatant signs and symptoms that they missed when the regressed pedophile was abusing the child. They are furious with themselves for not recognizing the danger their children were facing. Regressed pedophiles, however, have a façade that engenders trust among adults and an amazing ability to keep their victims quiet.

SILENT PARTNERS AND CO-PERPETRATORS

During the many years of MASA's existence, I have spoken with very few mothers who support husbands accused of sexually abusing their children. Most mothers who seek help at our office are already separated or divorced from the accused father, and trying desperately to protect their children through the court system. However, there is a subculture of non-offending parents who defend their accused spouses and actually accuse their own children of lying.

Decades ago, mothers could not protect their children; their very livelihood depended on the continuation of the marriage. Women did not work, and had no way to support their families. Caught in financial bondage, they looked the other way and ignored the abuse, or faced the abuser and suffered poverty.

Back then, the non-offending mother also had to face hostility and disbelief from her community. She and her child had little chance of being helped or even given credence by family, friends, religious leaders or social-welfare agencies. Consequently, she became a silent partner, or co-conspirator, to the perpetrator. Her inability or unwillingness to take action gave silent countenance to the pedophile.

A CASE HISTORY

In 1992, when MASA was first founded, Mary Kenney contacted our office to ask for our help because a family friend had molested her daughter, then a teenager. This close, trusted friend—the girl's godfather, in fact—taught band at her daughter's school and was a revered member of their community.

Mary learned about the abuse when she accidentally listened in on a telephone conversation, and subsequently read her daughter's diary. The abuse had been going on for many years, since the daughter was a little girl.

Mary confronted the predator by telephone while recording the conversation. Since the abuse had happened several years earlier and the predator knew the statute of limitations had run out, he opened up and bragged that he had targeted his godchild from the day she was born. He was confrontational and combative, claiming he was in love with the daughter and that the feelings were reciprocal. In fact, he admitted everything, and elaborated on the incidences of abuse.

In 1994, MASA supported new legislation to eliminate the statute of limitations for criminal prosecution in incest and child-sexual-abuse cases. It took several years for this new law to take effect, but when it did a few years later, it put Mary's case into a whole new arena. She filed a civil suit on behalf of her daughter, and won. As of this book, the daughter, now an adult has not pressed criminal charges, but she has that opportunity in the future.

Although the perpetrator in this case was held accountable in civil court, his wife stuck by her abusive husband, a silent partner to his crime. In fact, the process of disclosing this one case helped several other victims come forward, including some of his own family members. Yet even when faced with unequivocal proof that her own children, grandchildren and other relatives had been abused by her spouse, the wife remained loyal. She put her own needs and wants ahead of the safety and security of her own family.

Psychologists call this co-dependence—which, of course, it is. In my opinion, however, a person who willingly turns a blind eye to the abuse and devastation of her own children is a co-conspirator. By her silence and tacit support, she enables and facilitates the destruction of young, innocent lives.

What could make an adult be so callous about the health and welfare of a child? From a psychological perspective, denial ranks very high. From an empathy-for-the-child-victim standpoint, I believe such aiding and abetting of a pedophile constitutes child abuse in-and-of-itself.

Pedophiles and their conspirators should both be prosecuted to the fullest extent of the law.

Most people are shocked to learn about female child molesters. We have no hard statistics on how many women sexually abuse children, but scattered studies indicate that one in every thirty-five child-sexual-abuse incidents involved a female perpetrator. Because women are the traditional child caregivers, female molestation is far more difficult to detect than male molestation.

The betrayal and damage of mother-child incest is almost incalculable. No doubt one of the reasons we do not have more concrete data on these predators is the extreme shame the victim feels from this kind of violation. Several adult survivors have told me they were positive no one would believe them. Many female survivors sexually abused by other females end up very confused about their own sexuality. Their depression and low self-esteem take many years of therapy to heal.

Historical research describes women who sexually abuse children as deeply psychotic. More recent research reveals they might just as easily be well-educated, well-groomed professionals. Much like their male counterparts, they are almost impossible to identify or stereotype. What we know for sure is that they are serious predators, and should be held to the same standard of accountability as the male molester.

But they seldom are.

Consider the high-profile case of Mary Kay Latourneau, who not only sexually abused her student, but also had two children by him. Some may argue the boy was too old to be considered a child, but does anyone honestly think he was ready for the financial and emotional responsibilities of unwitting fatherhood? His teacher was in a position of responsibility and trust, which she clearly betrayed.

In a Pasadena, California case, a former mayor's wife was charged with sexually abusing several teenaged boys whom she entertained at her house. On her conviction, she was sentenced to probation and community service. At the same time, a male coach was charged with sexually abusing several teenaged boys. He was sentenced to eight years in jail.

MASA dealt with a case several years ago wherein eleven psychologists and other professionals substantiated that a mother had sexually abused her two young boys. Because social services did not substantiate the abuse and the judge simply could not bring himself to believe that a mother would molest her own children, she was never even charged! She retained custody for years until the father finally prevailed in court—after spending huge amounts of money, time and energy.

More Prevalent Than You Think

Over the years, many of my colleagues have treated both male and female survivors who had been sexually abused by their mothers. One significant female-abuser attribute they found was the level of physical abuse, such as excessive enemas and inserting foreign objects into the vagina or anus, that accompanied the fondling, digital (finger) penetration and oral copulation.

"Sarah" wanted to protect her young daughter from her own mother, who had sexually abused Sarah when she was a little girl. The grandmother denied the abuse had ever occurred. Sarah would not have been able to press criminal charges even if there had been corroborating witnesses because the statute of limitations had long passed. When the grandmother went to court to ask for grandparent's rights, Sarah turned to MASA.

We were able to support Sarah emotionally through the long court battle that followed. She presented many witnesses to her mother's sometimes very bizarre behavior. Thankfully, the judge found Sarah credible, and felt enough reasonable doubt about the grandmother's intentions and behavior to order professionally monitored visits. The grandmother soon lost interest with this kind of visitation, and Sarah and her daughter were able to move on with their lives.

As more data about females sexually abusing children becomes available, we will become better equipped to handle the cases. Until then, it will remain the perfect crime against children—and far more damaging even than male-perpetrated abuse.

Probably the most shocking revelation in recent years has been the magnitude of child sexual abuse allegedly committed by Catholic priests. How could so many men of God commit—or have been allowed by the hierarchy to commit—such heinous crimes against so many children?

The situation is almost impossible for non-Catholics to understand. As a person raised French Canadian Catholic, it challenges my own belief system. As a youngster, I was taught that priests and nuns were omnipotent. Parents considered it an honor when a priest took special interest in their child.

I was one of the lucky ones. In all the years of Catholic schooling, I was never approached or made a victim of anything untoward. I have long since converted to my own faith and belief system. Nevertheless, I feel betrayed by the actions and inactions of the Catholic clergy.

Over the years with MASA, I have worked with several clergy-abuse survivors. Most, but not all, were young men. While all child-sexual-abuse survivors have issues with trust, these victims were also ripped of their spirituality. The Father Llanos victims are prime examples.

Several young men in various stages of healing filed criminal charges against Llanos, who had repeatedly been reported for improprieties with children. But the California statute of limitations for criminal prosecution had expired and, consequently, the trial was discontinued and the charges dismissed. Father Llanos died by his own hand a few years later, leaving the survivors with no closure.

A civil suit was launched, to no avail. Since then, however, the statute of limitations for civil suit has been lifted, so hopefully, these young men will eventually have their day in court. They are not just looking for monetary compensation; they want—and deserve—a public apology from Llanos' superior, Cardinal Roger Mahoney. They want Mahoney to publicly admit that rather than protect the children in the Church, he protected Llanos and a number of other pedophile priests.

The scandal has been so huge that the Vatican approved a Zero Tolerance policy in the United States. Dedicated Bishops and Cardinals vowed to cooperate with investigating authorities, turn over offenders and let the United States justice system deal with the alleged abusers.

Unfortunately, not all in the Catholic hierarchy have, indeed, cooperated. As of this writing, cover-ups still exist, and clerical pedophiles are still being protected. In fact, nearly 200 U.S. Bishops are currently handling the scandals in their dioceses as they see fit.

FORMER GOVERNOR FRANK KEATING

In a rare move for the Catholic Church, Frank Keating, former Governor of Oklahoma, was appointed chairman of the Board of Lay Catholics and directed to look into the child-abuse scandal.

In his subsequent letter of resignation to Bishop Wilton Gregory, the president of the U.S. bishops, Keating compared Gregory's organization to *La Cosa Nostra*, saying "that is the model of a criminal organization, not my church."

His indictment caused a ripple of media coverage, followed by more denial and minimization from church officials. It is a wonder to me that Catholics can still support their parishes despite so many disclosures of child sexual abuse by their clergy.

MORE THAN THE CATHOLIC CHURCH

The Catholic Church is not alone in harboring pedophiles or covering up and minimizing sexual abuse by their clergy. Almost every denomination from Mormon to Seventh Day Adventists to Jehovah Witness, *et. al.*, have made headlines at one time or another exposing the child sexual abuse in their sects.

I have never understood how clergymen, the overseers of their flock, could ignore and minimize any child sexual abuse committed by one of their own. Yet, the clergy often vilifies these victims along with the congregations. Many survivors have told me their churches offered programs for the perpetrators—but not for the children or survivors!

In some cases, the perpetrator even asked the church body for forgiveness in a rather elaborate ceremony of recompense. The victim was forgotten; the person who had "sinned" received all the attention.

To me and many others, this is tantamount to sanctioning child sexual abuse. "Forgiving" pedophiles who pose as righteous, God-seeking people while scouting the availability of victims is beyond naïve or even ignorant, it is commensurate to aiding and abetting the abuse.

Ever church of every denomination must learn the facts about child sexual abuse. Churches must provide a safe environment for their adult and child congregants. Even a hint of inappropriate behavior toward children should impel the church to act immediately. The future of the church is not at stake; the futures of innocent children are.

Unfortunately, the majority of religions cover up and ignore the victims of child sexual abuse. Few denominations have escaped this vile reality. Churches must transfer their support from the "sinner" to the victims, and remember that forgiveness is a personal issue between the victim and the abuser—it should not be optioned by the church body, which insults the victim and minimizes the abuse. Only by holding perpetrators accountable can the victim receive validation.

The exposure of pedophiles in the Catholic Church is likely the tip of the iceberg. The Church is resistant to facing the problem.

Only the children have no options.

The Internet has transformed the entire world. Anyone with a computer that can go online can research and learn about almost any subject through this wonderful technology. It is information and instant communication at your fingertips, and the scope is almost limitless.

But, as with every human arena, the Internet has a dark side. Pedophiles can now contact child victims to fulfill their sexual perversions without fear of discovery. They can groom and entrap their unwitting victims while the child sits in the privacy and supposed safety of his or her own home.

Adult predators lurk in chat rooms and on message boards. The child, thinking he or she is talking to a same-age mate or friend, is a sitting duck for such con artists, especially when the parents are not Internet savvy. When parents have no idea to whom their child is talking with, pedophiles can easily recruit children into illicit and abusive relationships.

FAMOUS CASE

A woman in North Carolina who had endeared herself to a young man over the Internet arranged to meet with the fourteen-year-old boy at a pre-designated time and location. The boy went willingly, completely unaware of his "friend's" true identity or intentions. The woman and her husband abducted him and took him to another state, where they held him against his will and sexually violated him. Fortunately, smart police work rescued the child, returned him to his family in North Carolina and arrested the couple. The husband and wife now face prosecution for what has become a high-profile Internet kidnapping/molestation case.

But what about the cases that never reach the light and scrutiny of the media, the untold number of vulnerable children who may be involved with pedophiles and sworn to secrecy? It's anyone's guess how many cyberspace molestation incidents have not been discovered.

As yet, we have few laws governing the Internet, but studies indicate that over 60% of all websites are pornographic in nature. Cyber stalking has become a major issue of congressional debate, along with invasion-of-privacy issues, but the legislative process has not yet caught up with cyber predators. Law enforcement must be given the green light to not only identify Internet predators, but to arrest and prosecute them to the full extent of the law.

In the meantime, you as a parent must be pro-active about supervising your children and their chat-room and email companions.

- Know to whom your children are talking and what sites they view as they surf the Internet.

- Talk to your children about predators. Let them know that adults sometimes pose as children in chat rooms, on message boards and through e-mail.

- Tell your child to alert you immediately if he or she receives an e-mail or instant message from someone unknown.

- Caution your child to inform you if a chat-room conversation becomes suggestive or sexual.

- If you access the Internet through America-On-Line (AOL), sign up for their filter program that alerts you to unknown parties who may be communicating with your children. The program also blocks unknown users from having access to your children.

VOYEURISM

Voyeurism is a chronic disease or addiction, and very difficult to treat. Many adult survivors have told me their perpetrators gave them no privacy; they would catch the perpetrator spying when they were undressing or taking a bath. Voyeurism is covert sexual abuse that violates the victim whether or not anything physical takes place.

A 1994 American Psychiatric Association manual describes voyeurism as: "Symptoms that last over a period of six months, with recurrent, intense sexually arousing fantasies, sexual urges, or behaviors involving the act of observing an unsuspecting person who is naked, or in the process of disrobing, or engaging in sexual activity." More recent studies indicate voyeurism can be a precursor to physical assault, validating survivors' statements that, "At first, he just spied on me."

Make no mistake: voyeurism is not a victimless crime. Anytime a person invades the privacy of another person, child or an adult, it causes humiliation and shame. The victim's trust and feelings of safety are shattered. An insidious crime, it is often not reported simply because the victim is not aware it is reportable.

A 2003 John Walsh show revealed how a mother's live-in boyfriend had spied on her teenage daughter for seven years. He had installed a two-way mirror and video camera in the crawl space of their home with the camera aimed into the child's bedroom. The mother had not even been aware the crawl space existed. When discovered, it was littered with pornography and videotapes of her young daughter. He had even created a website on which he displayed the pictures.

For his crime, the perpetrator was ordered to stay away from the victim and her mother. For their victimization, the girl was permanently traumatized and the mother overwhelmed with guilt. The perpetrator won again.

We have no stereotypical profile for this kind of offender. He or she may be a loner lacking in social skills, incapable of having sexual needs met through normal channels. In the above case, however, the perpetrator had an apparently good and long relationship with the victim's mother. In other words, a voyeur could be anyone.

Voyeurs are often not terribly interested in pornography, even though voyeurism is about sexual arousal, because pornography involves professional actors willingly performing sexual acts. The voyeur is more interested in the covert aspect and humiliation he can cause his known victim. On the other hand, the media has reported incidences of two-way cameras in hotels, employee bathrooms and other locations that expose complete strangers in their private moments.

This is never a one-victim crime. If you have been the victim of a voyeur, call the police immediately. You may open the door for other victims to come forward. If the laws in your state are weak, contact your assemblyperson or senator and start working on a new law to make these perpetrators accountable. Seek therapy; many self-help groups and therapists are knowledgeable about this kind of abuse.

STALKING

Most stalking cases concern adults. In fact, according to Dr. Monica Lange, during a Cal State Long Beach lecture, "Up to 90% of women who are murdered in the United

States were stalked first. Stalking is a precursor to violence." Even if the stalking does not end in violence, it provokes such a great sense of terror that victims may be in therapy for years before they can reclaim their lives.

Stalkers who target children are one of the most dangerous and sometimes most brazen type of predators. In one upstate New York case, a 22-year-old neighbor stalked a seven-year-old child who lived across the street, terrorizing her whole family for six years. At first he began by stalking her in the family's swimming pool. Eventually, his flowers, love letters and little gifts escalated to threats over the telephone and letters in the family's mailbox. The family became concerned and notified the police. The police stepped up their patrols of the house, but could do little else. The man was finally arrested when the mother sat up several nights in a row and watched the mailbox. The stalker was ordered into a psychiatric hospital and away from the family. That ended the abuse, but did nothing to alleviate the damage to the family's sense of safety and security.

Stalking is not just a male crime; female stalkers are often just as dangerous as men. In fact, there is no set profile for adults who commit this crime. They may be dual-diagnosed and suffer from several mental illnesses or be the average person next store. They all exhibit some common symptoms, however, such as delusions and a need for power and control. The stalker often fantasizes that the victim wants a relationship. If the victim has recently severed a relationship with the stalker, the stalker may be bent on revenge. Whatever the circumstances, this is one crime that should never be underestimated.

In Stopping A Stalker (Plenum Publishing Corporation, 1998), Captain Robert L. Snow warns potential victims to act immediately if they believe they are being stalked. Contact law enforcement and ask for as much protection as possible. Change your telephone number if you are receiving phone threats and be vigilant in parking lots and other areas where you are most vulnerable. Weapons are not a good idea, as you could be providing the weapon for your attacker. If you carry mace, know how to use it. As a parent, be ever vigilant about knowing where your child is and with whom they are interacting.

Since 1993, I have been telling colleagues and friends that the movement to make pedophilia an alternate lifestyle is upon us. They have uniformly reacted with vehement denial and outrage, assuring me that good folks would never let this happen.

Well, good folks, you had better become pro-activists and advocates for child victims of sexual abuse, because it is already happening. You see, since 1993, I have been studiously watching Wardell Pomeroy and his agenda to gain support around the country.

As I was going through my normal avalanche of mail after returning from a 1993 Conference in Washington, I noticed an article enclosed in a long white envelope, no return address, titled:

Pedophilia Steps Into The Daylight

"Leading sex researchers and educators are touting the "benefits" of adult-child sex and are calling for more studies to prove it."

Written by Wardell Pomeroy, sex researcher and author of Boys and Sex and Girls and Sex (Dalacourt Press 1991), the article stated:

"I can say that this can be a loving and thoughtful responsible sexual activity.

"Pedophiles are adults who perform sex with children ranging from infants to teen-agers. Most are men attracted to boys, but some adult men are attracted to girls, and some adult women are attracted to boys."

Pomeroy is a founding board member of SIECUS, the Sex Information and Educational Council of the U.S., a private organization that writes guidelines many public schools use for their sex-education curriculum. Its bi-monthly report discusses developments in the field and offers teacher resources. In referring to pedophilia, co-founder and former president Mary S. Calderone, M.D. (deceased) asserted, "It is not that it's a bad thing or a wicked thing, it just simply should not be part of life in general, right out on the sidewalk."

THEY'RE NOT ALONE

John Money, Ph.D., a retired John Hopkins University Hospital Professor of Medical Psychology and Pediatrics, says, "Most pedophiles should not be jailed.... Pedophilia should be viewed as a sexual orientation, not a disease disorder." Money describes relationships between boys ten and eleven years old and adult males in their early twenties and thirties as "not pathological." He goes on to say that the relationships must be consensual and mutually satisfying with genuine bonding.

How can a 10- or 11-year-old child have "consensual" sex? How is it possible that the adult is not the initiating party, and is not taking advantage of the child's naivete and vulnerability?

John Hopkins University Hospital declared, "Money's views are his opinion. He represents himself. What he says doesn't necessarily represent the university."

THERE'S MORE...

John DeCecco, a member of Paidika, (the European spelling), a pedophile magazine published in the Netherlands, teaches a course at San Francisco State University titled: "Variations of Sexual Behavior." DeCecco states: "I argue on the side of liberty and keeping doors open and options open....

"The decision should largely rest in the hands of the people who are entering into the relationship.... If I am twelve and I decide to have sex with a nineteen-year-old or a fifty-year-old, that is really a choice I have."

Wayne Dynes, Ph.D., agrees that children can benefit from sexual relationships with adults. A member of the editorial board of Paidika, Dynes is a little more circumspect than DeCecco; he feels there are some negatives to pedophilia. He joined Paidika, he states, to study the issue "in as unprejudiced a way as possible."

Another worldwide organization outspoken in their advocacy of sexual relationships between men and young boys is North American Man Boy Love Association (NAMBLA). NAMBLA publishes a newsletter to go along with its very descriptive website. NAMBLA's reassurance to young boys is, "Do not despair. Be true to your feelings. Times will change and your oppression will end."

AND YET MORE...

"In a step critics charge could result in decriminalizing sexual contact between adults and children, the American Psychiatric Association (APA) recently sponsored a symposium in which participants discussed the removal of pedophilia from an upcoming edition of the psychiatric manual of mental disorders."
—"Psychiatric Association Debates Lifting Pedophilia Taboo," Lawrence Morahan, Senior Staff Writer, CNSNews.com, June 11, 2003

Psychiatrists at the symposium also proposed removing such disorders as exhibitionism, fetishism, transvestitism, voyeurism and sadomasochism from the Diagnostic and Statistical Manual of Mental Orders (DSM). These sexual disorders, long recognized as mental illnesses, come under the heading of "paraphilias." Morahan quotes Linda Ames Nicolosi, NARTH publications director, as saying, "If pedophilia is deemed normal by psychiatrists, then how can it remain illegal? It will be a tough law to fight in court that it is against the law."

Nicolosi also stated that whether pedophilia should be judged "normal and unhealthy" is as much a moral question as a scientific one, in direct contradiction to an American Psychiatric Association (APA) pedophilia fact sheet that labels it criminal and immoral: "An adult who engages in sexual activity with a child is performing a criminal and immoral act that can never be considered normal or socially acceptable behavior."

Morahan goes on to quote from "DSM-IV-TR and the Paraphilias: An Argument for Removal," co-authored by Dr. Charles Moser of San Francisco's Institute for the Advanced Study of Human Sexuality and Peggy Kleinplatz of the University of Ottawa. The paper argues that people whose sexual interests are atypical, culturally forbidden or religiously proscribed should not necessarily be labeled mentally ill.

How many of the general population even know the American Psychiatric Association is considering these kinds of changes? Do we, as a society, want to wake up some morning to find our children have legally become fair game for sexual perverts?

WE ARE FIGHTING BACK

When a MASA member sent a NAMBLA magazine to me a few years ago requesting I do something to stop its publication, I could not help wondering how many of the pictures depicted real children. Since child rape is clearly against the law in every state, I wondered how such images could be shown, especially in legitimate bookstores. The publications were removed after we staged a boycott of a few bookstores, but no one was fooled; it was a temporary, limited-location solution at best.

In 1994, MASA supported proposed legislation to stop NAMBLA meetings from being held in a San Francisco public library, where children browsed and did their homework. We failed; the state legislation declared the library a public place and the NAMBLA meetings were allowed to continue.

Dr. Judith Reisman, wrote Kinsey, Sex and Fraud, The Indoctrination of a People (Huntington House, Lafayette, LA), exposing famed sex-researcher Dr. Kinsey and his experiments with young children. According to Reisman's book, Kinsey used data from adult males who had contact with 196 children ranging from two months to 15 years to claim that boys are sexual beings and could benefit from adult sexual contact regardless of their age.

Kinsey wrote, "There are cases of infants under a year of age who have learned the advantage of specific manipulation, sometimes as a result of being manipulated by older persons."

YOU CAN FIGHT BACK, TOO

The movement to sanction sexual contact between adults and children is not about "civil rights." It is an attempt to ride the wave of legitimate social change, and justify self-serving behavior that inflicts permanent damage on children too young to defend themselves or understand the life-long ramifications of "consent."

In a democracy, a highly vocal minority can drown the will of the silent majority out. We who are dedicated to protecting the innocence of children must be aware and take advantage of the same freedoms of speech and legal remedies being used by sexual predators across the country.

- Groups advocating that the age of consent between adults and children for sexual relationships be lowered, in some states to age 12, must be stopped. If this is happening in your state, organize a letter-writing campaign in support of any legislator who boycotts such self-serving bills and let those who plan to vote "yes" know that you will fight them and their reelection publicly and aggressively. This is not a matter of civil rights. Whose rights do such laws look out for? Certainly not the children's.

- Boycott the products and companies whose television commercials depict children as less than childlike; e.g., wearing skimpy costumes and make-up.

- Prevention is step one: encourage your children to develop and maintain same-age friends and mates.

- Enforcing current law is step two: when 13- to 15-year-old girls have children by men in their late twenties and thirties, those men are guilty of statutory rape, regardless of the girls' consent, and the state is generally left to support the young mother and her offspring. If you know of any such case, insist that the man be prosecuted to the full extent of the law.

- Protest all overtures, whether legislative or by individual groups, that enable adults to have easier access to our children via the Internet.

- Exert your voice in every situation where you see exploitation of children. Complacency is not an option when you consider the ramifications of allowing predators to have legal access to abuse your children. If our courts ever sanction sexual relations between adults and children, our grandchildren and great-grandchildren will have no safety standards whatsoever.

Whether labeled as mental illness, religious taboo or societal abomination, the act of an adult emotionally, psychologically and/or physically harming a child in any and all forms must remain legally disallowed.

TEACH YOUR CHILD

The optimum solution to child sexual abuse is to prevent it from ever happening. You are your child's first and most important teacher. We readily teach our children to look both ways before they cross the road, never get into a stranger's car, don't take candy from strangers. Those are all important lessons, but today's children need far more safety education.

Child psychologists acknowledge that age two is not too soon to begin teaching children about their private parts in a non-threatening manner. Explain private parts as being any part of the body that a bathing suit covers. Do not frighten your children, but teach them that no one is allowed to touch their private parts. No adult is ever allowed to touch them with their private parts.

Let them know that if someone tries to touch their private parts, they are to tell you immediately. You can make this a game by role-playing. Have them practice shouting, "NO!" really loud to any adult who tries to touch them. Some pedophiles will back off immediately if they experience any resistance.

As they get older, teach them the correct names of their anatomical parts. Call a penis a penis, a vagina a vagina—there is no shame in these words, and you do not want your children to be ashamed of their bodies.

Most of us teach our children to be polite to adults, and it is important to have nice manners.

However, you need to teach your children that not all adults are nice people. If an adult makes them feel "icky" or "uncomfortable," they need to tell you.

Sometimes we inadvertently set our children up. Never force your child to give any adult a kiss or a hug. Never encourage your child to sit on an adult's lap. Let the child decide with whom he/she feels comfortable being affectionate. Children are people, only smaller. They have their own little built-in antennae, and are very capable of setting their own boundaries.

Tell your child it is okay to not keep a secret if that secret is about their private parts. Your child should also learn that an adult who wants to have a "special relationship" that involves either the child's or the adult's private parts is not acceptable. He or she should tell you immediately if any adult suggests such a thing.

WATCH YOUR CHILD

It cannot be said enough: be very careful when an adult shows an excessive interest in your child. I am not talking about doting grandparents. Still, let the child orchestrate his/her own affectionate gestures even with these close relatives. Healthy hugs and other gestures of affection are extremely important for children. Simply allow your child to set the pace.

Do not leave young children unattended even in their own yards. An adult or a substantially older sibling should be in attendance at all times. A case in California made headlines when a child was kidnapped off her own porch, raped and murdered. It has happened in other areas of the country as well. Parents cannot be too careful.

If you have to use a public restroom, take your child with you. Wait outside the door for children who are a little older and can go to the restroom alone. If an inordinate time seems to pass and you don't want to go into the opposite gender's restroom, ask an adult entering the facility to check on your child. Children are known to dawdle, but so are predators.

Be vigilant about what your child watches on television. Some programs are not appropriate even if they are geared for young children. Violence and adult language are not suitable for young children.

Be extremely cautious about which movies you let your older children see. Watching violence desensitizes children, and may lead them to think the behavior is acceptable. Sexually explicit scenes can influence a child into thinking that, too, is acceptable. Children are far more impressionable than we sometimes like to think. It is our responsibility to protect without smothering.

CHOOSING A DAYCARE

A wonderful daycare will encourage early learning while emphasizing social-skill development. Daycare can be a great benefit for young children, providing a good foundation for starting school. But before you decide on any particular daycare facility, do a little investigation.

Speak with other parents whose children attend the daycare. Find out what they like and do not like about it. Choose a facility with an open-visitation policy. If you cannot drop in to see your child at any time, look for another daycare.

Call your state's daycare governing board to see if there have been any complaints against the facility you're considering. Expect your child to have some separation anxiety the first few times you leave him/her, but if the behavior persists or your child starts to show fear about attending, re-scrutinize the facility.

Listen carefully to what your child reports. Red flags would be any kind of corporal punishment, inappropriate touching even by another child, scolding that seems irrational for the infraction committed, bruises, cuts, a sudden fear of the bathroom, nightmares, bedwetting and any other kind of unusual behavior that the child was not exhibiting before attending the daycare.

READ AND TALK TO YOUR CHILD

You can find many wonderful little books in your local bookstore or library that address child sexual abuse in an educational, non-threatening manner. Read them to or with your children.

Some schools have prevention programs that teach children how to protect themselves against sexual abuse. The Boy Scouts of America offer a prevention handbook for parents as well as an open policy to report any kind of abuse to their scoutmaster. More organizations, including preschools, now do thorough background checks on anyone who might come into contact with children.

Do not be afraid to talk with your child about sex. Many parents never received any concrete information from their own parents about sex, so they're squeamish when it comes to discussing it with their children. Remember, though, that your kids will learn about it one way or another. Would you rather they hear the real facts from you, or half-truths and nonsense from classmates, friends, the Internet or a potential predator? Knowledge is always power. Don't keep your children ignorant about sex; it could cost them their childhood or even their lives.

Children today are exposed to so much more and mature so much earlier than most of us did, but you still need to keep the information you relay age-appropriate. They need to know how babies are conceived, and that having a sexual relationship is appropriate for adults, but not for children. Explain the consequences of juvenile sexual encounters, including unwanted pregnancy, sexually transmitted diseases and emotional confusion and distress. It is not enough to just say "Don't do it" to today's teenagers, who see everyone "doing it" in TV shows, movies, books, magazines and newspapers. You must give them good, concrete reasons to refrain.

Prepare yourself to not display shock or condemnation so you can encourage the kind of open relationship with your child in which he or she can tell you anything. This is one of the most difficult things for a parent to do, but showing any kind of judgmental behavior will cause most children to simply clam up. No matter what your child is doing, you want to be the first to know so you can help both of you cope.

I may be criticized for this last bit of advice about older children who are sexually active, but I believe it is sensible: try to dissuade him or her from continuing to have sex. Quite honestly, it will probably not work. Once an individual embarks on a sexual life, biology takes over and stopping would be physiologically and emotionally abnormal. Nevertheless, that individual is still a child, and you are still the parent—who must now make an agonizing decision. Is it better to give your children the tools to protect them from unwanted pregnancy and sexually transmitted disease, or to play Russian roulette and hope that nothing bad happens?

As always, I opt for protecting the child.

Educate your children about the different methods of birth control and safe sex. Ask your family doctor to explain various methods and the side effects that may be involved. Be very aware of the age of the person your child is seeing. Remember: child sexual abuse occurs when there is a five-year or greater age difference. A 22-year-old having sex with a 14-year-old of either gender is statutory rape in every state in the union.

CHILD BEAUTY CONTESTS AND OTHER
EVENTS:

Pedophiles flock to events that involve
children, plain and simple. Beauty contests are just
one example. Does that mean all such activities
should be stopped? Of course not! What it means
is that you must be alert to who is taking special
notice of your children. Since pedophiles are virtually unrecognizable in society, make certain you or
a trusted adult is with your child at all times.
Again: pedophiles are cunning and clever con artists. Their ability to manipulate children is an evil
art, and they can manipulate adults as well.

A common pedophile ruse for luring your
child into a compromising situation is to pose as a
photographer, film producer or movie agent. Such
persons do frequent beauty, talent and sports
events, so it is not impossible that the person is authentic and sees great promise in your child. Any
parent would be flattered by that kind of attention.

Nevertheless, take no chances. Ask for more
credentials than just a business card. Personally
check the individual's references; a legitimate
show-business agent, photographer or producer
will not mind this scrutiny. Check the Internet to
see if the person has been convicted of child sexual
abuse.

Never, ever let your child go off with someone you do not know. An 11-year-old in Toronto,
Canada, was allowed to meet a "photographer"

who attended a gymnastic event at the child's school. Toronto is a very safe city and the "photographer" met the parents at the school—he seemed to be an upstanding professional. The child was raped and murdered.

Never let your guard down. Never.

PLAYGROUNDS, FAIRS, CARNIVALS, AMUSEMENT PARKS

Pedophiles often obtain jobs that put them in close proximity to children, and public areas that cater to fun for children are fertile ground for establishing contacts with potential victims. You cannot deny older children outings with their friends to participate in fun activities, but you can have some safeguards in place to protect them.

Always be sure your child adheres to the "buddy" system; that is, he or she will stay with at least one person all of the time, even when going to the restroom. Talk to all the children before they leave for the outing. Make sure both you and they have the telephone numbers of an adult who will be home and available to pick up them up if they run into any problem.

Never let them go with a stranger, no matter how friendly the person seems. Make sure they know that if a stranger says he has been sent by the parents to pick them up or says the parents have been in an accident, they should immediately call for verification—if you're not home, they should call another trusted family member or friend. If they cannot reach anyone they know—and in this day of cell phones, text messaging and instant radio access, that's not a likely occurrence—they should call security or the police, or use public transportation rather than take a ride with a complete stranger.

If you are attending an outdoor event with your younger children, keep them within your sight at all times. If you are tending to several children, make a chain by each child holding the next one's hand. Such precautions may sound overly strict or fun-imposing, but in today's world, pedophiles are bold and aggressive. A parent cannot be too careful.

SHOPPING MALLS

Shopping malls are often hangouts for pedophiles. As always, keep young children close to you. Some malls offer supervised babysitting areas where parents can leave their children so they can shop unencumbered, but even here I would advise caution. Make certain the adult supervisor knows exactly whom your child is. You can even make up a little identification kit with your child's photo and give that to the supervisor. Explain to your child about how long you intend to be gone, and that he or she is to stay within the perimeters of the play area.

Do not let your older children go to the mall alone. Ask them what stores they intend to visit so you have some idea where they'll be. If your child is going to drive or be driven, make sure they understand some simple parking-lot safety precautions:

- Do not park next to a van. A predator can open the door, grab a child and close it before anyone can stop him/her.

- Look around to make sure no one is near when opening the door to get in or out.

- Lock the doors immediately once inside.

- Do not dawdle in the lot, even with the doors locked and the windows closed. Make sure all seatbelts are secured, then pull or back out and leave the lot.

Teach your children that they can call home collect, even without money. If they have a cell phone, remind them to keep it charged, and to turn it on when they leave the house.

You cannot reinforce enough that your children must ALWAYS tell you where they are going. Teenagers, especially, feel they are invincible: walking the line between protecting them and letting them grow, experience life and learn to make their own decisions is never easy. Having fun is a natural and necessary part of life.

Making sure that fun does not end in tragedy is the awesome responsibility parents carry in today's society.

YOUTH ORGANIZATIONS

Youth organizations that teach integrity, sportsmanship and other life skills are invaluable: Boy Scouts, Girl Scouts, Little League, Boys and Girls Clubs, Big Brothers and Big Sisters, the YMCA—the list is ever growing. Most of the adults who spearhead these organizations are dedicated and conscientious child advocates. But as in all good things, the insidious pedophile may ingratiate him- or herself into these organizations to prey on innocent victims.

Pedophiles have almost a sixth sense for seeking out their victims. They know how to spot vulnerable children, especially the loners and shy ones. A common pedophile modus operandi (MO) is to befriend the child and sometimes part of or the entire family. Once the pedophile starts to feel confident, he or she begins the grooming process, which can range from tickling or back rubs to sexual conversations or showing the child pornography. The pedophile will offer incentives, such as showering the child with gifts, allowing him or her to drive an automobile, taking the child on trips and repeatedly reassuring the child that the pedophile is his or her only friend.

Making a child feel special is an art form with pedophiles, and leads easily to swearing the child to secrecy. Threats are rarely involved—by that point, they're seldom needed. The pedophile that befriends lonely children can wield more power and control through manipulation. Their victims keep the secret because they feel they may lose their "best friend." A lonely child is a virtual sitting duck for predators. Many come from one-parent homes where the custodial parent holds down a full-time job, but empirical evidence shows pedophiles are very successful at infiltrating families of any and every size and structure. Children can be insecure, vulnerable and lonely no matter how many parents are in the home.

SINGLE MOTHERS BEWARE

Since MASA's inception, literally hundreds of single mothers have contacted me because their boyfriends or live-in lovers have sexually molested their children. I cannot say enough words of caution to single women with children: do not allow the men you are dating to have access to your children.

It is hard to think that your new-found romantic interest is actually not as interested in you as in seeking access to your children, but it can be an absolute reality. Single moms who discover this betrayal seldom overcome the guilt at having exposed their child to such danger and degradation.

Holding a live-in partner accountable and filing criminal charges is rarely successful, and often comes back to haunt the mother. In many cases, the biological father immediately files for custody and the mother, guilty only of poor judgment, is suddenly faced with charges of failure-to-protect and child endangerment along with a custody battle. Even if the biological father does not come forward, the Department of Social Services may take the children into foster care. No matter what happens, the mother pays a high price for her choices. Ironically, the perpetrator will likely receive nothing more than a slap on the wrist, if that.

A FINAL WORD

Parental warnings could fill another book, and in some cases, they have. Please see Recommended Readings in the back of this book.

The old adage, "forewarned is forearmed," applies today more than ever. Parents must educate themselves, then educate their children. At times it can be a dichotomy; how can you raise free and healthy children while warning them about all the dangers lurking in today's society?

Just do it.

Arm yourself with every bit of knowledge available. Set boundaries for your child's activities and behaviors, and be involved in every aspect of their lives. Establish a support system with parents, teachers, coaches and others who are strong influences on them.

Growing up free of abuse is not a privilege, it is a right. No society can be healthy when it lets one out of every three girls and one out of every four boys be sexually abused before they reach 18. The children must become a priority in any nation that hopes to survive and thrive. Healthy children must be allowed to grow into healthy adults in order to maintain the integrity and peace of the world as a whole.

Protecting the children means protecting the greatest natural resource of any country. Children are the world's future.

Since the late 1980s, I have promised many of my adult survivor friends that when I finally wrote a book, it would offer the hope and encouragement so important to them. This chapter is dedicated to those courageous men and women in various stages of recovery who were so hurt as little children.

LORETTA

The human spirit has a wonderful recovery mechanism. I recently made contact with Loretta Woodbury, an amazing woman who had been sexually abused by her father. While Wyoming has never had a statute of limitations for any crime, the charges against her father was the first under the state's late-date prosecution law. Subsequently, Loretta went to former California State Assemblywoman Paula Boland and asked her to introduce a similar bill in California.

But even when the case was over and her father had been sent to prison, Loretta's life was not joyous, because she remained angry. When she finally decided to do the work of healing, the results were fantastic. She even persevered when severe health problems could have been a setback in her recovery. Now she's going back to school to earn her masters degree in counseling so she can help others. Loretta is one of my heroines. I am ecstatic about her recovery and dedication to helping others.

ALEX

Alex Lujan is another hero of mine. An adult survivor whose brother had perpetrated brutal sexual abuse against him while they were growing up, Alex served as my administrative assistant at MASA for several years.

Alex was very honest about being a recovering alcoholic and drug addict, and proved an inspiration to every person who met him at MASA. His compassion for survivors and non-offending parents garnered him a huge following. He was one of the first people to reach out in Alcoholics Anonymous and tell his story of child sexual abuse. Opening those floodgates enabled many other survivors to talk about their experiences.

Alex is about healing and moving on; his life exemplifies that living life to the fullest is not an impossible dream. Having done the work of healing, he serves as a beacon of recovery and reclaiming life. I am proud to be a small part of his.

CHARLENE

Another of my major heroes is my dearest friend, Charlene Marks. Charlene served as senior vice-president of MASA for over eight years. I am so honored to have been the first person to whom she confided about the child sexual abuse she had suffered at the hands of a neighbor. She did the work of healing and became the voice of validation and support for other adult survivors who contacted the organization.

I cannot possibly bestow enough accolades on this compassionate, understanding woman. Her ability to counsel adult survivors yet give them a good dose of tough love when necessary was nothing short of amazing. I felt blessed to have such a dedicated woman working beside me.

Charlene wrote and implemented MASA's teen-mother program. Many of these young mothers had been victims of incest as little children. Charlene did double duty administering to their recovery while teaching them parenting skills and important boundaries for their children. Schools across California wrote letters of appreciation, begging for more.

DONNA

Dr. Donna Friess, author of Cry The Darkness, is also a great heroine of mine. Her father sexually abused her and several other members of her family. When a young grandchild came forward and described her relationship with her grandfather, other family members began speaking about the abuse they, too, had experienced at his hands, and his father before him. They were shocked to learn so many family members had suffered in silence.

Although the statute of limitations had expired for Donna and most of her older relatives, everyone in the family joined forces to press charges against the father's most recent acts of child sexual abuse. They broke the generational cycle of abuse, and guaranteed the safety of their family's future children. The father died in prison raving that incest was sanctioned in the Bible, thus demonstrating once more how far perpetrators will go to rationalize their perversion.

Having received her doctorate long after she had healed from the wounds of incest and betrayal, Donna is currently a successful college professor who serves on many committees that protect children. A most encouraging example of overcoming adversity and moving on, she has sat on the MASA Board of Directors for many years. Her recent books, such as Circle of Love, focus on living life to the fullest.

TERI

Teri James was raped by her father when she was very young. She became MASA's official photographer for our fundraising events, at which we honored such celebrities as Melissa Gilbert, her husband Bruce Boxlietner and Phyllis Diller, both on her 50 years in show business and her 80th birthday.

Teri's indomitable spirit always makes being in her company a positive experience. She is not only an accomplished photographer, but a talented poet and short-story writer as well. She uses gardening as therapy and self-growth, and has the greenest thumb of anyone I know. Everything blossoms in her presence, including the friends who are privileged to be a part of her life. Her essay, "Be A Victor," printed in the back of this book, has inspired many child-sexual-abuse adult survivors.

MELISSA AND SHARI

Melissa Gilbert has appeared in a number of films highlighting child sexual abuse, including Lifetime's The Shari Karney Story.

Now a respected attorney, real Shari Karney was sexually abused by her father. She was one of the people who fought so hard to increase the California statute of limitation for delayed discovery in cases of incest and child sexual abuse. She knew from personal experience that some victims are not able to connect their life's problems to the abuse they suffered as children, or simply do not remember the abuse until years afterwards. The new law gave victims legal redress to file civil suits against their perpetrators.

YOU CAN HEAL, TOO

These examples should serve as validation that healing and living well is the best revenge against incest and child-sexual-abuse perpetrators. You can only hold your perpetrator accountable when you have healed enough to face him or her. To be honest, most survivors are not looking to file criminal charges or civil suits. In fact, many have told me they would be grateful if the perpetrator would simply admit the abuse and say those three magic words, "I am sorry."

Thanks to the Internet, child-sexual-abuse survivors can talk freely and anonymously with other survivors, and receive support and encouragement from others who understand exactly how they feel. Many have found that reaching out to others in the child-sexual-abuse chat rooms invaluable and empowering. As more and more survivors unite, the nay-sayers will no longer be able to deny the reality of this crime against children, nor minimize its lifelong effects.

As a survivor, you can heal and reclaim your life. You can stop the generational cycle of incest. Holding the abuser in your family accountable is a huge step toward cleaning up the family's dynamics. All the dirty little secrets get thrown wide open when a child or adult survivor discloses incest.

If your family does not rally behind you to protect its children and hold the perpetrator accountable, search beyond your own relatives and find support systems that will provide the healthy boundaries and unconditional love that were, and are your birthright.

WORK FOR IT

Healing does not just happen; it can require thousands of hours in agonizing therapy, reliving the abuse suffered as a child. Healing means recognizing that, yes, not only was your childhood stolen, but so was a major part of your adult life as you recover from that childhood. But the beauty of the human spirit is its incentive to be whole again. Others have done it. You can, too. Don't give up.

If you are an adult survivor of child sexual abuse and you have never told anyone, start talking. You are not alone. Hands and hearts will reach out to you to help you recover. Remember, the perpetrator cannot take any more of your adulthood than you allow.

Don't allow even one second more.

This book has been the most difficult thing I have ever attempted. In the 11-year history of MOTHERS AGAINST SEXUAL ABUSE, I have listened to the most heartbreaking and egregious cases of abuse of children. The atrocities happening to our children across the country are not being addressed adequately in our courts of law or by our legislators. If the health and safety of children is not a priority in this country, how will we ever secure a healthy society in the years to come?

Years ago, someone told me that since children are not a priority because they do not vote or pay taxes. I refuse to believe that—and I do not believe most responsible, thinking people hold that attitude. Certainly we are better than that; with education, we are more than capable of changing the future for child-sexual-abuse victims and holding their tormentors accountable.

I have worked for many years toward this end, and thanks to other child advocates, I have not been alone in my crusade. Dedicated adults and organization heads have endeavored to educate the courts that hold the very future and destiny of our children in their hands.

Judges today who negate critical evidence must be educated to the Signs and Symptoms of Abuse. They need to consider little children's disclosures as a major part of the evidence, and apply a little reverse reasonable doubt: how could three-

or four-year-olds describe oral sex, sodomy and other sexual acts unless they had experienced those acts?

If it takes a village to raise a child, it takes a nation to protect the children. In a country that offers so much to all its citizens, the very least we should provide for our future— our children—is safety. Nothing less is acceptable in a civilized society that seeks endurance and qualified leadership.

TERESA A. JAMES

Why stop at being a survivor? Many of us have been survivors of soul-rending acts for years and have learned that while that is a vital step on our healing path, we don't want to live there. We don't have to. Being a victor is our reward for all of our hard work, and that means that we can now simply BE.

Be that person your child-self once dreamed of being before the perpetrator took you deep into his or her dungeon of depravity. Be the doctor who heals others or the lawyer in court or the mother who nourishes and teaches our future generation. Be the artist who shares truths and joys with the world or the photojournalist who documents the world. In two words, BE YOU!

As survivors, we have the tools for the new growth necessary for the next step. We have already applied those tools for numerous stages of self-exploration and growth to date. This is simply another stage, the winner's stage. We learned in the survivor stage that although there are similarities in the methods of healing, there are various ways to implement those methods. The same is true for the victor stage.

For some, the answer lies in sending their perpetrator to jail. For others, that is only the beginning of surviving. For still others, like myself, the answer is forgiveness. I know this may seem impossible for many, and that is all right. Only you can decide what works best for you. I forgave my perpetrator for my benefit, not his.

In the act of forgiveness, I shifted the weight of carrying the burden from my shoulders back to where it truly belonged in the first place. Yes, I spent many years on my healing path prior to the day I wrote that letter of forgiveness. I realized that he still has to answer to his God or the Creator or Buddha at the moment of his departure from this world. Meanwhile, I have felt a freedom I never thought possible before.

I have returned to college to earn the rest of my long-postponed degree. I have enjoyed many loving years with my husband and two sons. I was capable of telling those I love and value about my past instead of hiding in the closet as if I were the perpetrator of my own crisis rather than the victim. I laugh and sometimes I cry, but now because of the present—not because of the past. In short, I live like most non-victimized individuals.

In 1981, Donald D'Haene was one of the first Canadian men to not only initiate prosecution of his molester, but go public with his story. His memoir, Father's Touch, is the first book in the world to detail his experience with sexual abuse within a Jehovah's Witness family.

An Associate Reviewer for Rebeccas-Reads.com, Donald just wrote, directed and starred in his first short comedy film, Viva Los Donald. Phat Puppy Productions has interpreted the first chapter of Father's Touch on film and in an original piece of music, while Toronto's Makin' Movies filmed a half-hour documentary of the story for Family Secrets on the W Network, directed by Genie-award-winning Maureen Judge.

TO OTHER MALE SURVIVORS OF CHILD SEXUAL ABUSE:

As a survivor of eleven years of child sexual abuse plus the trial in a very public case, what strikes me most ironic is that even in this new millennium, if you are a male victim, you more likely than not remain nameless, ashamed of your own experience.

You shouldn't be.

I have talked to over a thousand victims in the last two decades. Why should we be ashamed when our numbers are legion?

It's time we talked openly about our experiences with child sexual abuse. I have for over twenty years, and I've never felt so normal in my life.

It all began more than two decades ago, when I and four other victims (three male, one female) decided to charge our abuser. I asked the media to use my name. At that time, that was unheard of. Males didn't charge males for sexual abuse, let alone talk about their experience. Since then, of the scores of men who have disclosed their abuse to me, relatively few have yet gone public. Yes—for every man like hockey player Sheldon Kennedy, there are thousands who remain silent. Why?

Our society cultivates feelings of shame in subtle and not-so-subtle ways. Often, abusers are enabled to continue molesting by members of the community.

Consider, for example, the protection that powerful institution, the church, provided our abuser, my father. My younger brother disclosed the abuse to our mother. Two years later, my older brother confided in the ministers of our congregation. Reporting to the police would have involved the Children's Aid Society, which would have removed us from our father's reach. Although he was excommunicated by the congregation and our mother publicly reproved for not reporting the incidents to the ministers earlier, we four children were sent back home with our abuser. The congregation was protected—we, the abused children, and the public-at-large were not.

SANCTIFIED ABUSE

Sending us home with our abuser only isolated us further. His shame became our shame. What should have been labeled a crime was instead called "a sin."

My siblings and I agree that, as disgusting as the sexual abuse was, the worst thing our abuser did was mete out psychological anguish and torture. Our molester father, after all, was the person who had introduced God to us. It made us feel like God approved of the abuse, that this is what fathers were supposed to do. That monster made us feel as if we deserved it, wanted it, initiated it all—so, yes, we blamed ourselves. We thought the abuse was normal, and that we weren't.

Can you relate to those feelings? From the personal disclosures many other men have shared with me, my experience is not unusual in this regard. Our personal issues of shame and lack of esteem contribute to our silence.

Our abusers count on it.

Even people who truly cared nevertheless magnified our feelings of shame. One minister and his wife told me it would be better if I changed my name, "because there is a bad sound to it now. It's connected to the abuser. People will think of him, not of you as his victim."

Another reason for silence is a concern for the extended family's feelings. How did their feelings get to be more important than our own?

Disclosure may lessen your feelings of shame. How many times have you listened to your abuser being praised as a fine pillar in the community?

Our collective silence perpetuates abuse.

I am not suggesting that court proceedings will not prove daunting. In our case, even though a conviction was achieved, I learned justice is a relative term. The judge, in his oral reasons for judgment, said, my "childhood must have been a hell on Earth," but he also found that my abuser, "is not now, in my opinion, in need of rehabilitation or reformation, and is not now a danger to any member of the public." He based this on my father's lawyers' submissions and a psychiatric report that "shows clearly there is no overt sign of mental illness."

How is it possible that a victim's recovery process involves years of therapy about ongoing issues such as sexual confusion and flashbacks, whereas an abuser can be deemed free of mental illness, and not in need of rehabilitation in a matter of months?

In our case, the prosecutor never interviewed the victims or asked if we wanted to testify. He had arranged a plea-bargain before the case went to trial. We had no opportunity to dispute or challenge any testimony.

But I believe the most common reason male victims feel shame is our culture's imposed guilt on any homosexual contact. Unfortunately, sexual abuse of males is often labeled this way instead of as the criminal act it is.

What would I say to any child who contemplates bringing their errant parent to justice? Disclose the abuse not only to validate your own experience, but also to prevent the molester from continuing to abuse others. Speak with someone you believe you can confide in, such as a guidance counselor at school. If you are computer literate, search the Internet for information & material regarding sexual abuse and sexual-abuse hotlines, including toll-free phone numbers to call for help.

"But I'm not a child," you say. "That happened years ago!"

Unfortunately, time is not the great healer people hail it as. People ask me if time and my positive outlook have exorcised the demons of my past. Instead of exorcising "the demon," I found it was healthier to replace it with loving people who positively reinforce my self-worth, never discount my experience and allow me to be imperfect, angry, forgiving—whatever and whoever I am. The "demon" is a constant reminder of my resilience and will to live.

You must know where you've come from to appreciate where you are and where you want to be.

USE THE LAW

In many ways, charging abusers is one small step toward taking control of your destiny, of truly exorcising the demon. It may, in fact, work out to be a very empowering experience. In my case, my abuser as well as my peers considered me the least likely person to pursue justice. I went from being a weak wallflower to exerting an extraverted, charismatic, dominant force. From a mouse to a mouse-that-roars! I discovered I had a strength that everyone around me took for granted at best, and discounted and discouraged at worst.

If I did it, so can you. Don't underestimate yourself!

While each case must be considered individually based on your own needs, if you are considering charging your perpetrator, educate and prepare yourself for this harsh reality: the benefits of asserting oneself don't necessarily depend on happy outcomes, legal or otherwise.

After hearing countless victims' tales, attending several court cases and witnessing many survivors' disappointing experiences with people of faith, I really don't think things have changed enough in the two decades since our trial. Molesters still get a slap on the wrist, victims still receive stigma and shame and religion still provides a haven for a molester's reign of terror.

I recommend you receive extensive therapy before you even consider charging your abuser. Unless you have a strong and loving peer-support system in place, the process can be just another experience with abuse.

Whether you pursue avenues of justice or not, tell your story. But be selective. Many people will say the wrong things—count on it. Tell your story to a therapist or social worker, if possible. If you don't feel comfortable with one, find another. Their experience and objectivity will save you much heartache.

I can't stress this strongly enough: educate yourself. Fortify your knowledge with good therapy. Avoid people who don't validate your feelings.

Even though I have put a very public face on "male survivor," my quest for inner-peace continues. Me, myself and I have found relative success. I am more childlike than I ever was as a boy. Sometimes I catch a glimpse of the innocent sparkle I possessed as a toddler. Other times, I feel the innocence I never had during the rest of my childhood.

Now, in the maturity of my years, I am enjoying myself. I allow the full rainbow of emotions into my life. Yes, color me Donald! I laugh, cry, yell, scream, you name it. I do it. Free a caged bird and what does it do? It sings and it soars. I am free. Free at last.

If I can do it, you can too!

MOVING ON, GIVING BACK

I feel fortunate to have people in my life who care about me, love me and support me. On good days, such love envelops me. Fortunately, the good days are many, the bad few.

So if I'm so happy, if I have such a great future to look forward to and someone to share it with, why bother continuing to tell my story?

Because too many remain silent, unable to find their way out of the darkness. Because education and awareness empowers victims and weakens predators. Because if just one victim sees himself in me, realizes he is not alone, not to blame, has nothing to be ashamed of and can live a successful, productive and happy life, my disclosure will have been worthwhile.

Every one of us is unique, but we are all affected in one way or another: fear of intimacy, depression, compulsive or self-destructive behavior, insomnia, nightmares, flashbacks—the list is endless. Denying the past is not as healthy as some people proselytize, and unfortunately, many who tried haven't survived. They opted out on life because they could no longer bare the strain, the shame and the denial. Our collective stories and experience may help prevent future sad endings.

You can't escape the past; you have to learn to live with it. Survival is a never-ending process.

I encourage you, fellow victims and survivors, to take charge of your destiny. Come forward, seek help and healing. Tell your story and seek legal counsel now. Only through public bonding can we truly feel we are not alone, not to blame and do not need to continue feeling shame.

It has been an honor to work with Claire Reeves and be a small part of Childhood Should Not Hurt.

Indeed—It Should Not.

Donald D'Haene, June 26, 2003

Email:donald@fatherstouch.com

Author site: http://www.fatherstouch.com.

PART I

I WAS SEXUALLY ABUSED AS A CHILD. SHOULD I GO INTO THERAPY?

Most child-sexual-abuse survivors do need therapy at some time in their lives. You must do an inventory of your life today. If you are sad, having relationship difficulties, making compulsive decisions, thinking about the abuse more and more, experiencing sexual dysfunction or escaping into substance abuse, then seek therapy.

WHAT CAN I EXPECT FROM THERAPY?

You will address in a safe and compassionate environment what happened to you as a child. Your feelings will be validated. Your present behavior and subsequent problems will be validated by a professional who understands the trauma of child sexual abuse.

HOW DO I CHOOSE A THERAPIST?

Look for a therapist in the same way you would investigate a major purchase. The chemistry between the two of you is most important. Call a rape-crisis center or an organization that specializes in child sexual abuse for referrals. Friends who are also adult survivors may have recommendations. Do not depend on the yellow pages—not all therapists are child-sexual-abuse experts.

WHO SHOULD I TELL ABOUT MY ABUSE?

That is entirely up to you. Do not put yourself in a position where the abuse will be minimized. Many survivors hear, "Forget it; go on with your life." If you were sexually abused by a family member and that person is still alive, you may want to warn other family members who have children. Don't be lured into complacency and think the perpetrator will not abuse another child. This abuse is usually generational, and will go on for decades until one victim has the courage to speak up and stop it.

WHAT IF MY PERPETRATOR IS TOO OLD TO ABUSE ANOTHER CHILD?

Don't count on it. At the very least, find out if there are other victims so they can receive treatment. Elderly perpetrators still commit child sexual abuse. The perpetrator should be held accountable no matter what his or her age.

HOW DO I HANDLE THE FACT THAT MY MOTHER KNEW ABOUT THE ABUSE AND DID NOT STOP IT?

This is always so sad, but remember, years ago there was no education regarding incest and child sexual abuse. In fact, she may have been abused herself, and felt as helpless about you as she did when she was a child.

Today, we have information available about the devastating effects this kind of abuse has on a child. You could condemn your mother and let yourself dwell on the double betrayal, or you can deal with her inadequacies in therapy and realize that, for whatever reason, she is a handicapped and fearful person who simply was not up to the task of protective motherhood. Spending time and energy on hating someone because they are not who you want or need them to be only hurts you, and wastes your precious life resources.

SHOULD I FORGIVE MY PERPETRATOR?

Forgiveness is a very personal issue, and is entirely up to you. Never minimize the abuse for the sake of forgiveness; that could interfere with your healing process. If you were the victim of incest, you may be ostracized by the rest of your family for speaking up—but don't let that stop you. Talk to your therapist for help in coming to terms with your dysfunctional family.

PART II

WHAT IS THE DIFFERENCE BETWEEN CRIMINAL AND CIVIL COURT?

First and foremost, the evidence necessary to convict! In a criminal court, the evidence must prove guilt beyond a reasonable doubt. The verdict must be unanimous. Civil-court convictions are based upon a preponderance of evidence and do not require 100% unanimity of the jurors. A civil trial is actually an easier route to a conviction. O. J. Simpson was found not guilty in criminal court, but guilty in a civil wrongful-death trial.

HOW DO THESE COURTS APPLY TO CHILD MOLESTERS?

In a criminal trial, the evidence presented must persuade the jury beyond a reasonable doubt that the defendant is guilty. If convicted, the perpetrator could face prison.

Civil suits are about damages, not incarceration. If the jury finds against the perpetrator, the plaintiff will receive a monetary award. Collecting that award is a matter for the courts and your attorney, not the prison system.

WILL MY CHILD'S MOLESTER GO TO JAIL?

Statistically, no! According to the Department of Justice, less than 3% of child-sexual-abuse cases are prosecuted nationwide. Reasons include the age of the victim, the family's refusal to participate, a lack of corroborating witnesses, the perpetrator's age and clean record and the district attorney's lack of conviction the case is prosecutable.

MY CHILD'S ABUSER HAS BEEN CHARGED. WHY IS IT TAKING SO LONG?

The criminal justice system does not work quickly. Be patient. The accused has his/her own attorney, who knows how to work the system with one continuation after another. The longer the defense attorney can stall, the better for the defendant, especially if he or she is free on bail. Witnesses may change their minds about testifying, evidence could get lost, any number of things could happen to buy the accused time and freedom.

As the victims, you and your child are witnesses for the state. Ideally, the DA should keep you informed about what is happening in your case, but District Attorneys handle huge caseloads so keeping witnesses informed is not one of their highest priorities. Take responsibility for staying on top of your own case. Call the DA's office on a regular basis and ask the disposition of your case.

WHY WON'T THE DISTRICT ATTORNEY FILE CHARGES IN MY CHILD'S CASE?

In a perfect world, all criminals would be held accountable and punished for their crimes, but as we all know, this is not a perfect world.

Many district attorneys refuse to put children six and under on the stand, either because they don't think the child will be a good witness, or because they don't want to cause the child further trauma. Many district attorneys will not go to trial unless they are sure of a conviction. If the case comes down to the child's word against the adult's with no physical or corroborating evidence, the DA has little chance of conviction.

WHAT ABOUT CASES OF INCEST?

Incest cases are the least likely to go to trial. Our society seems to consider what happens in the family as family-only business. Families are considered sacred ground. That attitude has fostered and even condoned incest for generations.

To break the cycle, we need to re-examine what constitutes a family. If a parent or other family member is raping a child, that family should not qualify for "hands-off" treatment. Children should not be treated as chattel owned by the parents. They are little people who deserve the rights of any other American—and safety is one of those rights.

WE FAILED IN THE CRIMINAL TRIAL. SHOULD WE SUE CIVALLY?

That is completely up to you, and must be decided on an instance-by-instance basis. Any case is harder to prove in civil court if it failed in criminal court, but as the OJ Simpson trial clearly showed, success is not impossible.

SHOULD WE CALL THE POLICE IF WE LEARN OUR CHILD HAS BEEN SEXUALLY ABUSED?

Child sexual abuse is a crime in every state in this country. Many law-enforcement officers are specially trained in interviewing victims; however, many are not. You might want to take your child to his/her pediatrician first, and/or to a psychologist knowledgeable about child sexual abuse. Any professional you contact will be required to report the incident to your county's social-service agency. A social worker will then interview your child to substantiate the abuse.

WHY WON'T THE POLICE TAKE A REPORT IN MY CASE?

If you are an adult survivor, the statute of limitations may have run out. The early 21st Century Catholic Church scandal is a good example. Many of the crimes happened too long ago to be prosecutable.

HOW CAN WE HELP THE DISTRICT ATTORNEY PROSECUTE OUR CASE?

Most perpetrators abuse more than one victim, especially in the case of incest. Families must rally together to find the other victims and allow them to come forward without feeling shame and blame. This is not a matter of disloyalty to the perpetrating family member, but a question of loyalty to the victims and the integrity of the family.

HOW CAN I HELP THE COURTS SENTENCE MY ABUSER?

Most states allow victim-impact statements, which are very powerful and definitely influence judges' sentencing decisions. Do not be afraid to show emotion. Write the statement in advance and present it from your heart. You have the right to be outraged about such a crime, whether against yourself or your child.

WHY DID MY CHILD'S PERPETRATOR RECEIVE SUCH A LIGHT SENTENCE?

Every court of law is different. Was this the perpetrator's first offense? More likely, it was probably just the first time he/she was caught, but opinions are not evidence and only prior convictions are taken into consideration when sentencing is imposed. When the perpetrator has no priors, the sentence will likely be much lighter.

The defendant's age is also considered, as is the seriousness of the abuse and the victim's age. There is simply no concrete rule of thumb to predict the outcome of a child molester's sentencing. No matter what the sentence imposed is, children will be safer as long as the perpetrator is incarcerated.

DOES IT HELP IF I APPEAR AT PAROLE HEARINGS FOR ME OR MY CHILD'S ABUSER?

It not only helps, it is your right. You should appear at parole hearings with your witness statement and enlist the help of organizations that oppose early release of sexual predators. MASA has written thousands of letters to parole boards requesting parole be denied for sexual abusers. The boards take all this information into consideration. The recidivism rate for these kinds of offenders is well known. Keeping just one behind bars could save many children.

WHAT IS A PLEA BARGAIN?

A compromise for all parties, a plea bargain is an agreement made between the defendant, the defendant's attorney and the District Attorney's office to avoid trial and allow the defendant to plead guilty, usually to a lesser charge.

WHY DO THEY ALLOW PLEA BARGAINING IN CHILD SEXUAL ABUSE CASES?

Plea-bargaining is a standard legal device used to clear the court's backlog of cases. Plea bargains allow the victim to avoid the trauma of having to testify, yet see a form of justice prevail. The district attorney gets a conviction in a case even if he/she felt the evidence would not have persuaded a jury. The state saves the expense of a costly criminal trial. And the perpetrator, especially a first-offender, typically gets a lighter sentence than if convicted by a jury.

On the downside, these light sentences for first offenders are shortsighted. The recidivism rate is so high that the state will undoubtedly have to spend the same money and more to convict the individual in a later case. Meanwhile, the perpetrator is freed early to commit the same crime against other children.

WHAT CAN I DO TO HELP THE CRIMINAL PROSECUTION?

First and foremost, get the proper therapeutic help for the child victim. The more healed he/she is, the better chance that his/her testimony will be heard and believed.

Cooperate completely with the DA's office. Attend every hearing, even if you are told you do not have to attend. Pack the courtroom with friends and advocates for the child. All these things make a statement that you and many others are outraged, and that you expect justice to prevail.

WHAT IF OUR CASE SEEMS TO BE MINIMIZED BY THE COURT?

Turn to the media. Find a sympathetic journalist and spill your story. Judges are appointed or elected—either way, the judiciary is a very political arena. They are not going to want to appear soft on adults who sexually violate children. Recruit friends, family and child-advocacy groups and make your appearance known. Sometimes external pressure is the only thing that works.

WHAT IF MY CHILD'S MOLESTER BEATS THE SYSTEM?

If all is lost in criminal court, remember you can still sue in civil court. This is an agonizing decision for most parents—and the child's age is a big consideration—but it is an option.

NEVER consider taking justice into your own hands. You cannot protect your child if you end up in jail.

GENERAL GUIDES

Allender, Dan. B. Ph.D. *The Wounded Heart.* NavPress Publications, 1990.

Armstrong, Louise. *Kiss Daddy Goodnight.* Hawthorn Books, Inc., 1978.

Beatie, Melody. *Codependent No More.* Harper/Hazeldon, 1987.

Bennett, Jeffrey P. *Breaking the Bonds of Child Abuse – A Guide to Political Action.* Self-published, 1995.

Betts, Arlene H. A *Precious Resource – Teaching Personal Safety.* Westwind Press, 1999.

Bradshaw, John. *Bradshaw on The Family.* Health Communications, Inc., 1988.

Bradshaw, John. *Creating Love – The Next Great Stage of Growth.* Bantam Books, 1992.

Brady, Katherine. *Father's Days.* Harper & Row, 1979.

Carner, Talia. *Puppet Child.* PageFree Publishing, 2002.

Carnes, Patrick, Ph.D. *Out of the Shadows.* Hazelden, 1994.

Castillo, Roger, Jr. *Not With My Child.* United Youth Security, 1999.

Cermack, Timmen L., MD. *A Time to Heal: The Road to Recovery for Adult Children of Alcoholics.* Avon Books, 1989.

Crewdson, John. By *Silence Betrayed*. Harper & Row, 1988.

Faller, K.C. *Ritual Abuse: A Review of Research*. APSAC Advisor. Spring, 1994.

Feldman, G.C. Lessons *in Evil, Lessons From the Light: A True Story of Satanic Abuse and Spiritual Healing*. Crown Publishers, 1993.

Fraser, G.A. *The Dilemma of Ritual Abuse: Cautions and Guides for Therapists*. Washington, DC. American Psychiatric Press, Inc., 1997.

Fraser, Sylvia. *My Father's House*. Tichnor-Fields, 1987.

Fredrickson, Renee, Ph.D. *Repressed Memories*. Simon & Schuster, 1992.

Friess, Donna L., Ph.D. *Cry The Darkness*. Health Communications, Inc., 1995.

Fuller, A. Kenneth, M.D. *Unacceptable Risk: Child Sexual Abuse and AIDS*. Thomas College Press, 1998.

Furniss, Tilman. *The Multi-Professional Handbook of Child Sexual Abuse*. Routlege-Routlege, Chapman and Hall, Inc., 1991.

Gil, Eliana, Ph.D. *Outgrowing the Pain Together*. Dell Publishing, 1992.

Graber, Ken, M.A. *Ghosts in the Bedroom – A Guide for Partners of Incest Survivors*. Health Communications, Inc., 1991.

Haene, Donald D. *Father's Touch*. Millennial Mind Publishing.

Imber-Black, Evan. Ph.D. *The Secret Life of Families*. Bantam Books, 1998.

Korchin, Sheldon J. *Modern Clinical Psychology*. Basic Books, Inc., 1976.

Mones, Paul, J.D. *When A Child Kills – Abused Children Who Kill Their Parents*. Simon & Schuster, 1991.

John E. B. Myers, J.D. *The Backlash – Child Protection Under Fire*. Sage Publications, 1994.

John E. B. Myers, J.D. *A Mother's Nightmare – Incest*. Sage Publications, 1997.

Neddermeyer, Dorothy M. *If I'd Only Known...Sexual Abuse in or Out of the Family: A Guide to Prevention*. Millennial Mind Publishing, 2000.

Noblitt, Jr. and Perskin, P.S. *Cult and Ritual Abuse: it's History, Anthropology, and Recent Discovery in Contemporary America*. Praeger Publising, 2000.

Peck, M. Scott, M.D. *The Road Less Traveled*. Simon & Schuster, 1978.

Ridings, K.C. *Facing the Brokeness*. Herald Press, 1991.

Roseman, Mark E., J.D. *You The Jury*. Seven Locks Press, 1997.

Rush, Florence. *The Best Kept Secret – Sexual Abuse of Children*. McGraw Hill, 1997.

Sakheim & S.E. Devine (eds.) *Out of Darkness: Exploring Satanism and Ritual Abuse*. Lexington Books.

Scott, Brenda. *Out of Control, Who's Watching Our Child Protection Agencies?* Huntington House Publishers, 1994.

Seryak, John M. *Dear Teacher If You Only Knew*. The Dear Teacher Project, 1997.

Shore, Kenneth, Ph.D. *Keeping Kids Safe*. Prentice Hall Press, 2001.

Snow, Robert, L. *Stopping a Stalker*. Plenum Press, 1998.

St. Clair, Moira S. *Abused Beyond Words*. Pathways Unlimited Publications, 1998.

St. Clair, Moira S. 365 *Empowering Ways to Move Beyond Abuse*. Pathways Unlimited Publications, 2000.

Vates, Kelly. *Shattered Innocence*. Evergreen Press, 2001.

Westerlund, Elaine. *Women's Sexuality After Childhood Incest*. W. W. Norton, 1992.

ADVOCATE WEB
Box 202961
Austin, TX 78720
E-mail: hope@advocateweb.org
URL: www.advocateweb.org

ASSOCIATION OF SEXUAL ABUSE PREVENTION PROFESSIONALS (ASAP)
Box 421
Kalamazoo, MI 49005
Phone: 616-349-9072

BALTIMORE CHILD ABUSE CENTER
Investigates all reported child sexual abuse cases in Baltimore, MD
10 South Street Suite 502
Baltimore, MD 21202
Phone: 410-396-5165

CHILD ABUSE PREVENTION PROGRAMS
Box 265
Dolton, IL 60419
Phone: 708-841-5414

CHILD ABUSE PREVENTION SERVICES
Phone: 708-841-5414

CHILDHELP USA
Child Abuse Survivor and Prevention Program
1345 El Centro Ave
Box 630
Hollywood, CA 90028

CHILDSAVERS, INC.
Prepares individuals for court appearances, informs them of their rights and teaches them effective strategies for dealing with situations they encounter as they attempt to protect children.
PO Box 10564
Rockville, MD 20849-0564
Phone: 301-251-9099

CHRISTIAN SURVIVORS OF SEXUAL ABUSE (CSSA)
BM-CSSA, London, WC1N 3XX UK
Contact: Margaret Kennedy

CLEARINGHOUSE: CHILD ABUSE PREVENTION
2314 Auburn Ave
Cincinnati, OH 45219
Phone: 513-721-8932

COALITION FOR ADVOCACY AND ACCURACY ABOUT ABUSE
Family Violence and Sexual Assault Institute
1310 Clinic Drive
Tyler, TX 75701

FOCUS ON THE FAMILY
Colorado Springs, CO 80995
Phone: 800-232-6459

FROM DARKNESS TO LIGHT
A non-profit organization that seeks to reduce the incidence of child sexual abuse by moving adults from awareness to advocacy. Their award-winning public-awareness campaign and highly-acclaimed educational products and programs teach how to better prevent, recognize and respond to child sexual abuse.
247 Meeting Street, Suite 200
Charleston, SC 29401
(843) 965-5444
URL: www.darkness2light.org
Email: darkness2light_2000@yahoo.com

GOOD TIDINGS
Box 283
Canadensis, PA 18235

Phone: 717-595-2705

ICASA (ILLINOIS COALITION AGAINST SEXUAL ASSAULT)
4708 Main Street Legal Office Suite 201
Lisle, IL 60532-1760
Phone: 708-971-9606

JUSTICE FOR CHILDREN
2600 Southwest Freeway, Ste #806
Houston, TX 77098
Phone: 713-225-4357
Fax: 713-225-2818
Email: info@jfcadvocacy.org

LaCASA
1 South Greenleaf St
Phone: 708-244-1187

LETSTALKCOUNSELING.COM
Email: Info@iofx.com

THE DEFENSE FOUNDATION FOR CHILDREN
PO Box 65
Losantville, IN 47354
Phone: 765-853-5903
Email: Dmarhoefer2@aol.com
Contact: Denise Marhoefer

SURVIVORS AND VICTIMS EMPOWERED (SAVE)
1725 Oregon Pike, Ste. #106
Lancaster, PA 17601
Phone: 717- 569-0550
Fax: 717-569-3039
URL: www.s-a-v-e.org

MOTHERS AGAINST SEXUAL ABUSE
PO Box 371
Huntersville, NC 28070
Phone: 704-895-0489
Email: Clairemasa@aol.com

Website: www.againstsexualabuse.com
Contact: Claire Reeves

NATIONAL CLEARINGHOUSE CENTER ON CHILD ABUSE & NEGLECT
Dept of Health and Human Services
Box 1182
Washington, DC 20013
Phone: 800-394-3366

NATIONAL COUNCIL ON CHILD ABUSE AND FAMILY VIOLENCE
1155 Connecticut Ave NW Suite 300
Washington DC 20036
Phone: 202-429-6695

NATIONAL ORGANIZATION FOR WOMEN
San Gabriel Chapter/Whittier Chapter
Phone: 626-297-5420

OUR LADY OF VICTORY TRUST - SERVANTS OF THE PARACLETE
Brownshill, Stroud GL6 8AS
England
Phone: direct dial from USA: 011440-1453-88-3084
Fax: direct dial from USA: 01144-1453-73-1888
e-mail: info@olvgranthill.freeserve.co.uk
Contact: Pam Perry

PREVENT CHILD ABUSE AMERICA
332 South Michigan Ave Suite 1600
Chicago IL 60604
Phone: 312-663-3520

PREVENTION INFORMATION RESOURCE CENTER
Federation on Child Abuse and Neglect
134 South Swan Street
Albany NY 12210
Phone: 518-445-1273

RAPE AND SEXUAL ABUSE CENTER OF MIDDLE TENNESSEE, INC
56 Lindsley Ave
Nashville TN 37210
Phone: 615-259-9055

SAFEHOUSE/SEXUAL ASSAULT SERVICES, INC
Box 1885
Cheyenne WY 82003
Phone: 307-637-7233

SASSY INC.
Sexual Abuse Survivors Support Year-round Inc.
PO Box 727
Rice Lake, WI 54868
Phone: 715-234-8445
URL: www.sassyinc.org
Email: info@sassyinc.org
Email: sistersurvivor@sassyinc.prg

SEXUAL ASSAULT SERVICES, INC. (SARA)
Box 16
Surrey BC V3T 4W4 Canada

SNAP
Survivors Network of those Abused by Priests
PO Box 438679
Chicago IL 60643-8679
Phone: 312-409-2720
URL: http: //www.snap-net.org/
Contact: Barbara Blaine

STOP IT NOW!
PO Box 495
Haydenville, MA 01039
Phone: 413-268-3096, Fax: 413-268-3098
Web: www.stopitnow.com
e-mail: info@stopitnow.com
Contact: Fran Henri

AUSTRALIA

LIFELINE
24 hrs Australia wide
13 11 14

New South Wales

RAPE CRISIS CENTRE
24 hours
1 800 424 017

ADVOCATES FOR SURVIVORS OF CHILD ABUSE (ASCA)
02 9840 4098, or 1 300 657 380

DYMPNA HOUSE
Child Sexual Assault & Resource Centre
1 800 654 119, or 02 9716 5100

SURVIVORS OF INCEST ANONYMOUS (SIA)
02 9692 0829

WOMEN'S INCEST SURVIVORS NETWORK (WISN)
02 9560 6627

Northern Territory

ALICE SPRINGS SEXUAL ASSAULT RESOURCE CENTRE
08 8951 5880

ROYAL DARWIN HOSPITAL, CASUARINA
08 8922 8888

RUBY CAEA HOUSE
Darwin Centre Against Rape
08 8945 0155

Queensland

BRISBANE RAPE & CRISIS CENTRE (BRICC)
24 hours
07 3844 4008

WOMENS HOUSE, HIGHGATE HILL
24 hours
07 3844 4008

CAIRNS RAPE CRISIS CENTRE
24 hours
07 4031 3590

SEXUAL ASSAULT SUPPORT SERVICE
Sunshine Coast & Gympie Region
07 5443 4334

South Australia

WOMEN'S HEALTH STATEWIDE
1 800 182 098

YARROW PLACE RAPE & SEXUAL ASSAULT SERVICE
1 800 817 421

SOUTHERN WOMEN'S HEALTH CENTRE
08 8384 9555

Tasmania

SEXUAL ASSAULT SUPPORT SERVICE
03 6231 1811

LAUREL HOUSE, LAUNCESTON
03 6334 2740

Victoria

CASA HOUSE ROYAL WOMENS HOSPITAL, CARLTON
03 9344 2210

DOMESTIC VIOLENCE & INCEST RESOURSE CENTRE, CARLTON
03 9387 9155

GEELONG RAPE CRISIS CENTRE
03 5222 4049
Western Australia

INCEST SURVIVORS ASSOCIATION
08 9227 8745

PRINCESS MARGARET HOSPITAL, SUBIACO
08 9340 8222

SEXUAL ASSAULT RESOURCE CENTRE
1800 199 888

WOMENS HEALTH CARE HOUSE, NORTHBRIDGE
08 9227 8122

USA

JUST FOR KIDS HOTLINE
1888 594 KIDS

CHILDHELP NATIONAL CHILD ABUSE HOTLINE
Voices for Children
24 hours
1800 4 A CHILD or 1800 422 4453 TDD: 1-800-2A-CHILD

CHILD ABUSE HOTLINE
Dept of Social Services
1800 342 3720

NATIONAL CHILD ABUSE HOTLINE
1800 792 5200

NATIONAL YOUTH CRISIS HOTLINE
24 hours
800 442 HOPE or 442-4673

SUICIDE PREVENTION HOTLINE
1800 827 7571

SPANISH DOMESTIC ABUSE HOTLINE
1800 942 6908

BELGIUM

THE CHILDREN AND YOUTH TELEPHONE
078 15 14 13

ELKE DAG TUSSEN 16 EN 20 UUR BEHALVE OP ZON-EN FEEST-DAGEN KINDER EN JONGERENTELEFOON- PROTECTION DE L'ENFANT KINDERBESCHERMING KINDERSCHULTZ

NUMEROS DE TELEPHONE IMPORTANTS !(FRANCAIS)
0800-14400 (n??? gratuit)

BELANGRIJKE TELEFOONNUMMERS! (DUTCH?NEDERLANDS)
078 15 14 13

WICHTIGE TELEFONNUMMERN (DEUTSCH)
087 74 49 59

BRITAIN (UK)

CHILDLINES HOTLINE
0800 1111

NSPCC CHILD PROTECTION HOTLINE
0800 800 500

YOUTH 2 YOUTH
0181 896 3675

CANADA

KIDS HELP PHONE JEUNESSE,JECOUTE
 (24 hours Toll Free anywhere in Canada)
1800 668 6868

DANMARK (DENMARK)

FORENINGEN STTTECENTER MOD INCEST I DANMARK
33110708 & 33330708 man - tor 15-21
Ung P-E5 Linie 31386666 man - fre kl-14-22, lr kl-14-17

BRNETELEFONEN 35555555 KL-12-19

DGNKONTAKTEN- 35373623

IRELAND

IRELAND CHILD HELP LINE BY ISPCC
1800 666 666

GARDA (POLICE) CONFIDENTIAL LINE
24 hours, Toll Free
1800 666 111

ISRAEL

ELEM
Hotline for youth under stress or in danger Tel Aviv
(03) 641 4508 or (03) 641 8792

ELI-SOCIETY PROTECTING THE KIDS
Toll Free
177-022-3966 (Toll Free)

MEITAL
The Israeli help center for sexually abused kids Yerushalayim
(02) 563 0428 or Tel Aviv (03) 525 3206

MAKOM ACHER
A safe house for kids who need it- Tel Aviv
(03) 517 6135 or (03) 517 6246

ERAN

PSYCHOLOGICAL FIRST AID DIAL 1201 ANYWHERE IN ISRAEL

SEXUAL ABUSE AND RAPE HOTLINE DIAL 1202 ANYWHERE IN ISRAEL

YOUTH HELP LINE
Milev center
02 654 1111 or toll free or 1800 654 111

KAV CHERUM
Emergency Hotline

ALIMUT BAMISHPACHA VI YILADIM BASIKUN
FAMILY VIOLENCE AND KIDS IN DANGER
1800 22 0000

ITALY

TELEFONO AZZURRO
1-96-96 numero gratuito riservato ai bambini

TELEFONO AZZURROROSA
030/226363 – 2420845

NETHERLANDS

HOTLINE FOR KIDS IN TROUBLE
(14: 00-20: 00 hrs everyday)
(+31) 06-0432

NEW ZEALAND

NO BULLY
For Kids being bullied
0800-NO-BULLY/0800-66-28-55

YOUTH LINE, 13 MAIDSTONE ST GREY LYNN AUCKLAND
09 3766 645

20 Putney way Manukau city Auckland
00 2639 400

RAPE CRISIS AUCKLAND
Po Box 105-241 Auckland central
09 3667 213

AUCKLAND SEXUAL ABUSE HELP, 2 CONWAY RD MT EDEN
09 6231 700

VICTIM SUPPORT
08 0084 2846

YOUTH SUICIDE AWARENESS TRUST
Po Box 3369 Auckland CLEAR Toll Free 0508

CHOOSE LIFE - SPINZ YOUTHLINE
Suicide Prevention for crisis support phone

YOUTHLINE
0800 376 633

ECPAT
International Secretariat
328 Phaya Thai Road
Bangkok Code: 10400
Tel: (662) 215-3388
Fax: (662) 215-8272
E-mail: info@ecpat.net
Url: http://www.ecpat.net

A nationally recognized expert in incest and child sexual abuse, Claire R. Reeves has testified in both civil and criminal cases. In 1992, she founded MOTHERS AGAINST SEXUAL ABUSE (MASA), a national non-profit organization dedicated to protecting children against sexual abuse.

As she spearheaded MASA, Claire also set up programs to assist non-offending parents and guardians of children who had been sexually abused. Her emotional support, compassion and knowledge helped them maneuver through the quagmire of the family and juvenile court systems.

Claire has appeared on numerous television and radio shows, and been profiled along with the organization in newspapers and magazines across the country. She is a sought-after speaker for conferences nationwide and has lectured at numerous universities, hospitals, social-service agencies and other organizations dedicated to preventing child sexual abuse.

Claire has been at the forefront on many of the new California laws that apply to child sexual abuse. She was actively involved in eliminating the statute of limitations for criminal prosecution, getting the chemical-castration law passed and establishing a 900-telephone hot line to identify registered sex offenders. For her tireless work, she has received honors from the Mayor of Los Angeles, the California Assembly, the California Senate and then-Governor Pete Wilson. In 1997, Claire Reeves was named a Los Angeles County Woman of the Year.

Claire's passion for child victims and adult survivors of sexual abuse is indomitable. Her goal is to implement national educational programs not only for parents, but even more for those who decide the fate of abused children. Education is the key to eliminating child sexual abuse, and the goal of *Childhood - It Should Not Hurt.*

While each of these signs can occur for a myriad of reasons, five or more unexplained changes of more than one type should raise the sexual-abuse red flag:

UNEXPLAINED PERSONALITY CHANGES

Becomes introverted or secretive

Loses interest in grades, sports, hobbies or other pastimes

Becomes secretive about source or reason for gifts or money

UNEXPLAINED BEHAVIOR CHANGES

Cries constantly

Has "accidents" in panties or bedclothes after potty trained

Wears multiple layers of clothes in all kinds of weather

Is afraid of or refuses to use the bathroom

Is afraid of certain adult(s)

Is afraid to go to sleep, or has constant nightmares and night terrors

Sleeps excessively

Knows more about sex than other same-age children

Acts out sexually with other children beyond age-appropriate curiosity

Acts out sexually with adults

Acts out sexually with dolls or other toys

Masturbates excessively, or tries to force foreign objects into vagina or anus

Uses a vibrator or other sexual paraphernalia (older children)

UNEXPLAINED PHYSICAL CHANGES

Ongoing vaginal infections

Sexually transmitted disease

Vaginal scarring
Pre-adolescent broken or detached hymen

DECLARATION

Discloses sexual abuse